ATHENIAN STUART

Pioneer of the Greek Revival

STUDIES IN ARCHITECTURE
Series editors: JOHN HARRIS and MARCUS BINNEY

ATHENIAN STUART

Pioneer of the Greek Revival

DAVID WATKIN

London
GEORGE ALLEN AND UNWIN
Boston   Sydney

George Allen & Unwin (Publishers) Ltd,
40 Museum Street, London WC1A 1LU, UK

George Allen & Unwin (Publishers) Ltd,
Park Lane, Hemel Hempstead, Herts HP2 4TE, UK

Allen & Unwin Inc.,
9 Winchester Terrace, Winchester, Mass 01890, USA

George Allen & Unwin Australia Pty Ltd,
8 Napier Street, North Sydney, NSW 2060, Australia

First published in 1982

British Library Cataloguing in Publication Data

Watkins, David.
   Athenian Stuart.
1. Stuart, James   2. Architects – Great Britain – Biography
I. Title
720′.092′4   NA997.S/
ISBN 0-04-720026-X
ISBN 0-04-720027-8 Pbk

Set in 11 on 13 point Sabon by Computape (Pickering) Ltd,
and printed in Great Britain
by William Clowes Ltd, Beccles and London

Contents

List of illustrations

Acknowledgments

I am grateful for help in various ways to Mr John Harris, Mr Brinsley Ford who allowed me to consult the papers of the Society of Dilettanti, Mr Hugh Pagan, Mr Roger White, Mr John Hardy, Miss Alison Kelly, Mrs Grace Holmes, Archivist to the Dean and Canons of Windsor, Miss Janet Smith of the Staffordshire Record Office, Dr Ian Fraser, Archivist of Keele University Library, Sir John Summerson and the staff of Sir John Soane's Museum, and the Librarian of the Huntington Art Gallery, San Marino, for permission to quote from documents in his care.

Photographic acknowledgments

British Library 15; Cambridge University Library 2; A. C. Cooper 47–50; Country Life 17, 26, 29–34, 36, 42, 44–6; Courtauld Institute of Art 18, 41, 43, 57, 79; A. Crowther 66–7; Dean and Canons of Windsor 80; Greater London Council Photograph Library 28, 51–3; Kedleston Archives 20–3; A. F. Kersting 6, 10; National Monuments Record 7, 9, 13, 16, 19, 54, 58–62, 64–5, 68–9, 73; Godfrey New 55–6; Pierpont Morgan Library 39–40, 78; Royal Institute of British Architects 1, 3–5, 18, 41, 43, 57, 63, 70, 72, 76; Sir John Soane's Museum 55–6; Warburg Institute 68–9, 71, 75, 77.

1 The Antiquities of Athens

James Stuart (1713–88), dubbed 'Athenian'[1] in his lifetime, must be accounted one of the great luminaries of eighteenth-century Europe inasmuch as it was he, more than anyone else, who opened men's eyes to the dignity and merit of Greek architecture. The impetus which led Stuart and Revett to publish measured drawings of buildings which had been unaccountably ignored for centuries was eventually to flower in the architectural products of the Greek Revival from Edinburgh to Corfu, from Moscow to Savannah.

Stuart's achievement as an archaeologist must be set historically in the context of the spirit of inquiry characteristic of the collectors, travellers and patrons who made up the Society of Dilettanti. This remarkable group of noblemen, gentlemen and amateurs began by founding a drunken dining club in 1732 and ended by making England for a hundred years a leading European centre for the study of classical archaeology and for the transformation of modern design through imitation of the forms and principles of antique art and architecture. It is this ambition of reforming modern design which gives a particular fascination to the career of James Stuart. Like his successors, William Wilkins (1778–1839) and C. R. Cockerell (1788–1863), who were also members of the Society of Dilettanti, archaeologists and architects, Stuart was confronted with the problem of applying his archaeological knowledge to the design of modern buildings, interior decoration and furniture. Whilst it could scarcely be claimed that Stuart's attempt was overwhelmingly successful, there can be no doubt that his particular kind of failure is of considerable interest. The failure, if such it be, was as much one of personality as of artistic capacity. Charming, idle and unreliable, he ended his days playing skittles in the afternoon and drinking in a public house in Leicester Square in the evening. During the fourteen years between his announcement of his Proposals for Publishing an Accurate Description of the Antiquities of Athens, and the publication of the first volume in 1762, he and Revett were beaten to it by David Le Roy (1724–1803) who, on reading their prospectus, rushed to Athens where he spent under three months but managed to produce *Les ruines des plus beaux monuments de la Grèce* in 1758. However, whatever the reality of the situation, it was believed in the late eighteenth and early nineteenth centuries that Stuart's revolution had been successful. James Elmes admitted of Stuart in 1847 that 'This eminent man was more of an artist than a practical architect', but nonetheless emphasised that 'No event that ever occurred in the history of architecture in England, and thence throughout all Europe, produced so sudden, decided, and beneficial effect as did the works of James Stuart.'[2]

Stuart was born in London in 1713 in Creed Lane, Ludgate Street, the son of a Scottish sailor. When his father died, the young James, showing a natural talent for drawing, found employment with Louis Goupy (1700–47), the well-known French fan-painter who had settled in London (Plate 1). He thereby helped support his mother, brother and two sisters. It may have been Goupy who aroused Stuart's interest in antiquity for he had accompanied Lord Burlington on his first Grand Tour of Italy and frequently decorated his fans with paintings of classical buildings. Following his mother's death, Stuart was able to fulfil his ambition of completing his artistic education in Rome. In 1742 he set out on foot for Rome where he quickly became a respected judge of pictures and was employed as a guide by English visitors. He learned the art of engraving and by 1749 was preparing engravings from his own drawings of a newly discovered Egyptian obelisk. These were published in Bandini's *De Obelisco Caesaris Augusti e Campi Martii ruderibus nuper eruto* (Rome 1750) together with an account of the obelisk (Plate 2) in the form of a letter by Stuart addressed to the Earl of Malton, afterwards Marquess of Rockingham and a future patron. The publication was subsidised by the archaeologically-minded Pope Benedict XIV, to whom Stuart was presented.

Stuart arrived in Rome at about the same time as Nicholas Revett (1720–1804), the son of a Suffolk squire, who studied painting under Marco Benefial, a minor artist of the Bolognese school. The two young men became friends and soon formed a group with Matthew Brettingham (1725–1803), who bought antique sculpture for Lords Leicester, Dartmouth and Egremont, and Gavin Hamilton (1723–98), the influential Scottish dealer, painter and collector. In April 1748 the four men made a tour to Naples in the course of which they first dreamed of making a full and scholarly record of the monuments of ancient Greece along the lines of Desgodetz's celebrated *Edifices antiques de Rome* of 1682. Desgodetz's book, which remained a standard source for nearly two centuries, had been commissioned by Colbert, founder of the Académie Royale d'Architecture, to enable French architects to have access to the correct models. Though Colbert sent agents armed with copies of Pausanias to Greece and the Levant to visit the ancient sites and to collect manuscripts, coins and medallions, he never thought of producing a Greek Desgodetz. In 1647 a French diplomat, the Marquis de Nointel, explored Athens and commissioned drawings of the Parthenon sculpture by Jacques Carrey. Inspired by notes compiled by J.-P. Babin which were sent back to France by Nointel, Jacob Spon left his native Lyons for Greece, financed by Colbert. In Venice he met the English botanist George Wheler and in 1676 published *Voyage d'Italie, de Dalmatie, de Grèce et du Levant* which contained the first published engraving of the Parthenon. This rather glum view was also published by Wheler in his *Journey into Greece* (1682), dedicated to King Charles II. Some measured drawings of the Parthenon appeared in Richard Pocock's *Description of the East and Some Other Countries* (1745), while five years later Jacques-Germain Soufflot and G.-P.-M. Dumont measured the Doric temples at Paestum though they did not publish the results until 1764.

Stuart and Revett's original prospectus, which we know from the summary of a lost letter from Revett to his father of January 1749, envisaged a work of three volumes. The first was to contain fifty-three views of Greece and its buildings; the second plans, elevations and architectural details accurately measured after the manner of Desgodetz; while the third would consist of sixty-seven plates of sculpture. The whole was to be completed in as little as four years, only one of which would be spent in Greece. Stuart and Revett would spend the remaining three years in England making engravings from their drawings. It is interesting to see how far the prospect of financial gain, however over-optimistically calculated, entered into the scheme of things. Revett estimated that 'the neat profit at the end of four years to the three Artists was, at the most *moderate compensation*, and after paying every expense while thus employed, to amount to ten thousand pounds.'[3]

The actual Proposal of 1748, as published in 1751, makes their aims so clear that it ought to be quoted at length:

There is perhaps no part of Europe more deservedly excites the Curiosity and Attention of the lovers of Polite Literature than the Province of Attica, and in particular Athens its capital City; whether we reflect on the figure it makes in History, on account of the excellent Men it has produced, or whether we consider the number of Antiquities still remaining there, monuments of the good sense and elevated genius of the Athenians, and the most perfect Models of what is excellent in Sculpture and Architecture...

Rome, who borrowed her Arts and frequently her Artificers from Greece, had by means of Serlio, Palladio, Santo Bartoli, and other ingenious men, preserved the memory of the most excellent Sculptures and magnificent Edifices which once adorned her; and though some of the originals are since destroyed, yet the memory, the exact form of these things, nay the Arts themselves seem secured from perishing, since the industry of these men have dispersed examples of them through all the Polite Nations of Europe.

But Athens, the mother of Elegance and Politeness, whose magnificence scarce yielded to that of Rome, and who for the beauties of a correct style must be allowed to surpass her, as much as an original excels a copy, has been almost completely neglected, and unless exact drawings from them

16

be speedily made, all her beauteous Fabricks, her Temples, her Theatres, her Palaces will drop into oblivion, and Posterity will have to reproach us...

We doubt not but a Work so much wanted will meet with the Approbation of all those Gentlemen who are lovers of Antiquity, or have a taste for what is excellent in these Arts, as we are assured that those Artists who aim at perfection must be infinitely more pleased, and better instructed, the nearer they can draw their examples from the fountain-head.[4]

Hamilton and Brettingham having dropped out of the enterprise for reasons that are not entirely clear, Stuart and Revett arrived in Venice in the spring of 1750. A note of realism now entered their proposals as they began to seek serious financial backing. They were fortunate in being supported by two members of the Society of Dilettanti living in Venice: Sir James Gray, British Resident, and Joseph Smith, British Consul. Gray organised a subscription list, introduced them to the Society of Dilettanti and proposed them for membership in 1751,[5] making them the first artist members of the society. Thus, if the Dilettanti Society made possible the achievement of Stuart and Revett, their election to it altered its character by giving it a new professional seriousness. Joseph Smith arranged for them to be protected in Greece by yet another member of the society, Sir James Porter, Ambassador at Constantinople. In the meantime Colonel George Gray, secretary and treasurer to the Dilettanti Society and brother to Sir James Gray, published Stuart and Revett's Proposals in London, while Consul Smith produced a further edition in Venice in 1753.

A precious survival from this period is a sketch-book by Stuart which was given to the RIBA by 1846. It contains about seventy sketches of buildings and views in north Italy, presumably made between March and July 1750 when Stuart was in Venice waiting for a passage to Athens. We find drawings of buildings by Palladio, Sansovino, Sanmicheli and Falconetto. Several sketches relate to the Villa Pisani at Stra (Plates 3, 4), a Baroque palace retaining some Palladian elements begun in 1735 for the Doge by Girolamo Frigimelica. Stuart was evidently impressed by its large hexastyle portico and a number of his sketches consist of proposals for a palace with domed end pavilions inspired by this building. The sketch-book also contains notes on Venetian painting and a draft for a treatise on the use of colour in painting. He was especially attracted by the chiaroscuro of the Venetian school whose painters he regarded as 'more attentive to please the eye than to touch the heart.' He thought their success lay in their control of 'light, shade, body, texture, hue and direction'.

Whilst waiting in Venice Stuart and Revett also made a valuable expedition to Pola in Dalmatia (Yugoslavia) to measure the two Roman temples, arch and amphitheatre. Their voyage, begun in July 1750, was made memorable by the presence of numerous live crabs in coarse canvas bags 'making a noise like the frying of fish, or the pattering of a heavy shower of rain.'[6] In 1753 Stuart and Revett's reconstruction of the Corinthian Temple of Rome and Augustus at Pola was made the basis of an unexecuted design by Colonel George Gray for the Dilettanti Society's proposed clubhouse in Cavendish Square.

It was not until February 1751 that Stuart and Revett finally left Venice for Greece. They arrived in Athens on 18 March where they found working conditions unfavourable and their lives endangered by plague and political upheavals. However, one inhabitant pulled down a house to enable them to get a proper view of the Tower of the Winds, though they seem to have rebuilt it afterwards. They spent two and a half years at their task, which compares favourably with Desgodetz's sixteen months in Rome, Le Roy's three months in Athens and the absurdly short space of nine days which Wood spent in Palmyra and Baalbek. Their meticulous and painstaking methods of measuring and recording caused them to be regarded as spies by both Greeks and Turks. It also meant that the Tower of the Winds and the Choragic Monument of Lysicrates were the only buildings which they had measured in accordance with their own highest standards. Thus in May 1754 they were proposing to include only these two buildings in the first volume and to return to Athens to make further measurements when political unrest was at an end. Happily the first volume, published in 1762, was not quite so drastically curtailed as had been envisaged eight years before. However, the six buildings it contained included none of the great Periclean masterpieces but were nearly all minor and later works dating from the Hellenistic period: the temple at Pola, and, in Athens, the Temple of Augustus, Choragic Monument of Lysicrates, Tower of the Winds, Stoa, and Temple on the River Ilissus, now destroyed. These did not provide a framework for a full-scale Greek Revival so that Winckelmann, who had expressed great interest in the original Proposals, complained in a letter of 1764 of the triviality of the buildings illustrated in the first volume. In the Advertisment to the second volume, written in 1787, Stuart explained that 'When Mr. Revett and I returned from Athens, and received Subscriptions for our first Volume, uncertain whether we should be encouraged to proceed farther with this Work, we selected such Buildings for our proposed publication, as would exhibit specimens of the several kinds of Columns in use among the ancient Greeks; that, if, contrary to our wishes, nothing more should be demanded of us concerning Athens, those who honoured us with their Subscriptions to that volume, might find in it something interesting on the different Grecian modes of decorating Buildings.'

This seems to imply that their ambition was now to enrich the stock of decorative motifs rather than to initiate a radical reform of architecture as a whole. Indeed, the major buildings of the Acropolis did not make their appearance until the second volume was published in 1789, the year after Stuart's death. This volume, which was largely due to the efforts of Stuart's assistant William Newton, contained not only the Parthenon, Erectheion and Propylaea but also the later Choragic Monument of Thrasyllus, Theatre of Bacchus and Temple of Jupiter Olympius. Concentrating in their illustrations on the decorative aspects of architecture, they tended to ignore technical considerations such as the use of clamps and dowels, and even the presence of entasis and horizontal curvature.

Stuart finally left Athens for Constantinople on 20 September 1753 but was nearly murdered by Turks on the way. He rejoined Revett in Salonica in April 1754 and together they revisited the Greek archipelago and the island of Delos. They returned to England via Smyrna and Marseilles, arriving home on 27 October 1755. They went to live with the traveller and

19

archaeologist James Dawkins at his house in London where they seem to have remained until his death in 1759. Their presence in London caused quite a stir. In 1761 Hogarth produced a caricature of 'The Five orders of PERRIWIGS ... measured Architectonically ... taken from the Statues, Bustos and Baso-Relievos of Athens, Palmira, Balbec and Rome'. Stuart pasted this engraving on his fire-screen and always showed it to visitors. In 1758 he was appointed Surveyor of Greenwich Hospital on the recommendation of his friend Lord Anson, and in 1763 became painter to the Society of Dilettanti. A fatal laziness was already discernible in Stuart with the result that he was replaced as the society's painter by Reynolds in 1769, having failed to fulfil his obligations. However, he exhibited watercolour drawings of Athens at the Free Society of Artists. Twenty of his attractive drawings in gouache, a technique he had learned from Goupy, survive at the RIBA Drawings Collection. These topographical views of classical antiquities in Athens (Plate 5), Salonica and Pola were all engraved in the four volumes of the *Antiquities of Athens*. Such colourful and essentially Picturesque impressions were Stuart's special contribution to the *Antiquities*, while the painstaking measured drawings were largely the work of Revett. Nonetheless, Stuart had bought out Revett's share of the publication and royalties probably before the appearance of the first volume in 1762.

We know from Stuart's Italian sketch-book of 1750 that he was particularly sensitive as a painter to qualities of colour, light, texture and reflection in painting. His surviving architectural drawings are sensitive impressionistic examples of a Picturesque technique which was one of the most attractive developments in the architectural draughtsmanship of eighteenth-century England. He was also aware of the intensity of light and shadow in Greek architecture produced by Greek sunlight. James Gandon, who knew him, said, 'Stuart frankly acknowledged that the fine blue sky, the constant sunshine, with the bleaching of the stone and marble to a pure white colour, combined with the exquisite beauty of the different existing remains of Grecian structures, combined to render their appearance truly impressive.'[7] The outline engravings produced from Revett's careful drawings naturally robbed Greek architecture of much of its intensity and vitality, making it seem chill, disembodied and colourless. In fact, it was precisely these qualities which Winckelmann admired in Greek art, for the discovery of the role of polychromy in Greek architecture and sculpture did not come until the early nineteenth century. Colour, Winckelmann wrote in his *History of Ancient Art* (1764), 'should have but little share in our consideration of beauty, because the essence of beauty consists not in colour but in shape, and on this point enlightened minds will at once agree'; great art should be flavourless like pure water. Despite his powerful advocacy of the merits of Greek art Winckelmann never visited Greece. Indeed, he turned down several opportunities of travelling there with all expenses paid, and instead envisaged Greek art in terms of the smooth forms of Raphael and the Apollo Belvedere. Just such an approach was encouraged by Stuart and Revett's engraving technique which, departing from the vigorous Baroque tradition, rendered sculpture with an even overall cross-hatching. Thus surface irregularities were smoothed out and replaced with the clear contours and generalised forms admired by Winckelmann. We know that Flaxman made tracings from Stuart and Revett and may have based the angels in his superb monument of 1784 to Mrs Morley in Gloucester Cathedral on their engravings of the flying figures on the Tower of the Winds in Athens.

Flaxman could not afford to buy the *Antiquities of Athens* until 1796. Indeed, if we look at the list of 500 subscribers to the first volume we find only four architects and three builders. This emphasises the fact that, in its promotion by a small clique of noblemen and connoisseurs, the new movement was no different from the successive Palladian revivals in England under Inigo Jones in the seventeenth century and Lord Burlington in the eighteenth. The only change was that there was now an established architectural profession, led by Sir William Chambers as Comptroller of the Works from 1769, able to defend itself against the Greek Revival which it saw as a potential threat. Thus, encouraged by Piranesi's well-known and polemical hostility to Greek architecture, the prolific architect James Paine wrote of Wood, Stuart and Revett in his *Plans, Elevations and Sections of Noblemen and Gentlemen's Houses* (1767) that 'It is a great pity ... that all trifling disputes among these gentlemen, about the different measurements of those antiquities, had not been entirely omitted; for, let their disputes be carried to what length they please, it will be of little consequence as the particular forms of the best examples among them, are scarcely one remove from the rude essays of the Egyptians, from whom the Greeks borrowed them.' He also argued that 'If in consequence of the acquirement of modern travelling knowledge, convenience and propriety are to be sacrificed to the modes of the most despicable ruins of ancient Greece, it is greatly to be lamented.'[8] Adam was no less hostile, at any rate in private conversation, while Chambers delivered lectures at the Royal Academy, known to us from his surviving manuscript notes of 1768, which contained an even more sustained and personal attack on Stuart and Revett. He claimed that 'a General Outcry of Artists and Connoisseurs would perhaps bring even the Gothic Architecture into Vogue again, and might cheat us into a reverence for Attic Deformity, but the Opinions of two or three or half a dozen can have but little weight in a matter of this Nature; they might with equal Success oppose a Hottentot and a Baboon to the Apollo and the Gladiator as set up Grecian architecture against the Roman.'[9] Chambers subsequently published this attack in the third edition of his *Treatise on Civil Architecture* in 1791, but by this time the writing was on the wall for the kind of dignified Palladian-cum-Louis XVI classicism which Chambers represented. Within a couple of decades the Greek Revival was to dominate English Architecture. However, this moment had certainly been delayed by the hostility of Paine, Chambers and Adam but also by Stuart and Revett's lack of determination and perhaps, in the end, lack of skill in translating their ideas and their knowledge into bricks and mortar.

2   Landscape architecture

The England to which Stuart returned in October 1755 was coloured architecturally by the movement which was to be the principal British contribution to European aesthetics: the Picturesque. As early as 1709 Vanbrugh had argued for the preservation of Woodstock Manor in the park at Blenheim not only for its interesting historical associations but because careful planting could make it resemble 'One of the Most Agreable Objects that the best of Landskip Painters can invent.'[10] From this moment the Picturesque became established as the characteristic eighteenth-century way of seeing. The result is the curious make-believe quality in which gardens look like paintings and buildings look like scenery: the role of association, the piquant contrast of styles and the recognition of growth and change, all became second nature to architects. It thus seems wholly appropriate that the first building designed by Stuart on his return from Greece should have been a garden building in the form of a Greek Doric temple gracing an eminence on the edge of the deliciously Rococo park of the 1st Lord Lyttelton at Hagley, Worcestershire. The scenic ability which Stuart showed in his topographical views of Athenian buildings was put to good effect in this picturesquely placed little building at Hagley (Plate 6) which, inspired by the Theseum in Athens, represents the end of a Doric hexastyle temple with a column at each side of the cella entrance behind the colonnade. It is built of red sandstone originally covered with stucco and commands superb views towards the Malvern Hills. This is important in showing that it was built as much with an eye for the views from it as for those towards it. This point is confirmed in a letter of October 1758 from Lord Lyttelton to the great blue-stocking Mrs Montagu: '[Stuart] is going to embellish one of the Hills with a true Attick

23

building, a Portico of six pillars, which will make a fine effect to my new house, and command a most beautiful view of the country.'[11]

As the first use of the fluted baseless Greek Doric order since the ancient world, Stuart's temple at Hagley is rightly hailed as a landmark in the history of European architecture. However, in France at exactly this moment J.-G. Soufflot (1713–80), who had studied the Greek temples at Paestum in 1750, was designing Greek Doric columns for the crypt of Ste Geneviève (today the Panthéon) in Paris. The contrast between the English and the French approach to the revolutionary Greek Doric order is instructive: the English is essentially pictorial, the French intellectual, inasmuch as a primitive order is considered by Soufflot to be especially appropriate as the foundation for a more elaborate superstructure. Though there are virtually no Greek Doric garden buildings in France, the theme of the Doric crypt recurs several times, the most notable surviving example being in the church of St Leu-St Gilles, Paris (1773–80) by Charles de Wailly (1730–98).

George, 1st Lord Lyttelton (1699–1773), secretary to Frederick, Prince of Wales, and briefly Chancellor of the Exchequer, was the valued friend of the leading poets and intellectuals of the day. The ideal patron, he was also a nephew of Lord Cobham whose extravagant endeavours in the park at Stowe inspired him to lay out a similar park at Hagley from the late 1740s. Thus to appreciate the full resonances of the temple at Hagley it is important to appreciate its role in the Rococo eclecticism of the house and park together with their respective contents. We know, for example, that Stuart, according to Lord Lyttelton, 'seems almost as fond of my hall as of the Thessala temple [the Theseum at Athens].'[12] The austere Palladian house at Hagley, designed for Lyttelton in 1754 by a committee of taste presided over by Sanderson Miller, contains interiors adorned with fine Rococo plasterwork by Francesco Vassalli. The hall, of which Stuart was so fond, contains not only Vassalli plasterwork but a chimney-piece carved by James Lovell flanked by straining atlantes, as well as copies of antique sculpture. The same mind, be it Lyttelton's or Stuart's, could appreciate simultaneously Greek sobriety, Rococo fantasy and even Gothic romance, for in

1747–8 Sanderson Miller built a ruined castle in the park at Hagley. This incorporated genuine medieval windows brought from the nearby Halesowen Abbey and, in Horace Walpole's oft-quoted comment, 'has the true rust of the baron's wars.'[13]

It was not, however, at Hagley that Stuart's gifts as a Picturesque designer of classical buildings were to be chiefly deployed, but at Shugborough, the Staffordshire estate of Thomas Anson (1695–1773), a bachelor, Whig MP and founder member of the Society of Dilettanti. Like his friend Lord Lyttelton, Anson was a man of considerable intellectual refinement. In 1740 he travelled in the Levant in the hope of collecting antiquities, but he was unable to indulge his artistic tastes to the full until he inherited a fortune on the death in 1762 of his younger brother, Admiral Lord Anson. In 1747 he and his brother had built a chinese house at Shugborough, an enchanting piece of Chippendale chinoiserie remotely inspired by drawings made in China by one of Admiral Anson's officers. At about this time the eccentric grotto designer, mathematician and astronomer Thomas Wright (1711–86) was employed by Anson to adorn the ground with Chinese, Gothic, primitivist and classical garden buildings including a fragmentary Doric colonnade. It was into this whimsically Rococo wonderland that Stuart, apparently without any sense of incongruity, dropped from *c.*1762 a chain of buildings which constitute a remarkable three-dimensional expression of the plates in the *Antiquities of Athens*. The first and most prominent of the Athenian monuments at Shugborough was the Triumphal Arch (Plate 7), modelled on the Arch of Hadrian (Plate 8), a Roman work in a stylistically somewhat Baroque taste. The masons submitted estimates in November 1761 but, following Admiral Anson's death six months later, the building became a memorial to him and his wife. Appropriate sculpture commemorating the man who had helped re-establish British naval supremacy was carved by Peter Scheemakers who, as late as June 1769, was modelling a medallion in which 'Neptune & Minerva are establishing naval discipline.'[14] Christopher Hussey has seen in such monuments something of the political symbolism which we know informed Lord Cobham's iconography in the gardens at Stowe. The Whig members of the Dilettanti Society especially admired the buildings of Athens where, they could argue, political liberty had been born.

In 1764 came two more souvenirs of Athens, the Tower of the Winds and the Lanthorn of Demosthenes. The former (Plate 9) is a simplified version of the Horologium of Andronikos Cyrrhestes and was originally surrounded by a lake with two Chinese bridges leading to the two porticos, while the latter is, of course, a copy of the Choragic Monument of Lysicrates which had been built in Athens to support the tripod won by a cyclic chorus in 334 BC (Plate 10). Stuart was obviously much attracted by the element of exuberant fantasy in the design and decoration of this building, the first in which Corinthian columns were employed outside (Plate 11). The original tripod and the bowl for libations which rested on it had both long since been lost, but Stuart made a clever and attractive restoration of them in volume 1 of the *Antiquities of Athens* (Plate 12). This he now translated into three-dimensional form at Shugborough, capping the monument with a handsome bronze tripod made at the Soho manufactory near Birmingham. Stuart wrote to Anson on 23 September 1769: 'The tripod is in great forwardness, I think it will be best to have it cast at Birmingham, my friend Mr Boulton will execute it there, better & cheaper far than it can be done in London. I will call on the artificial Stoneman tomorrow morning, the Freize [presumably painted] of the Lanthorn is advanced I shall bring it down to finish at Shugborough.'[15] Visiting Shugborough in 1770 Josiah Wedgwood found the workmen struggling to hoist Boulton's heavy tripod to the top of the monument and suggested that the surmounting bowl should be made of Wedgwood ware instead. Two experimental bowls were certainly made at the Wedgwood factory but it is not clear whether one was ever erected at Shugborough. The present tripod and bowl are fibre-glass reproductions made for the National Trust in 1965. The position of the building in the park seems to have been the choice of Anson rather than of Stuart whom we find writing rather touchingly to his patron in June 1764: 'Pray is the place for the Lanthorn of Demosthenes any where by the canal, & near the fine Clump of Trees just at the angle, pardon my inquisitiveness, I cant help thinking about it.'[16]

The curiosity value of these two Hellenistic buildings, the

Tower of the Winds and Choragic Monument of Lysicrates, made them popular with later eighteenth and early nineteenth-century architects such as Wyatt, Inwood and Elmes, and also with designers of funerary monuments. In *c.*1780 Stuart himself provided another copy of the Tower of the Winds in the park at Mount Stewart, Co. Down, while a rare French example was built at Plessis-Chamont later in the century. One of the most striking neo-Classical monuments in a Stuartian style is that in Ripon Cathedral to William Weddell (1736–92) who may have employed Stuart at Newby Hall. A bust of Weddell by Joseph Nollekens of 1789 is enshrined within an exquisitely detailed demi-rotunda inspired by the Choragic Monument of Lysicrates.

So far, all Stuart's buildings at Shugborough have been inspired by Hellenistic or Roman examples. It seems probable, therefore, that we can also attribute to him the design of a further three including the Doric Temple[17] which, with its hexastyle portico, is close to that at Hagley though less picturesquely sited. Stuart built an impressive orangery near the house in 1764, its skyline bristling with urns and its interiors painted by the Danish artist Nicholas Dall. On 25 September 1770 Stuart wrote to Anson:

Mr Dall has shewn me the design for the pictures in the green-house & library. The Subject for the Green house is a view of the temple of Minerva Polias with the Caryatides, on the principal ground, & in the distance he has introduced what remains of the Odeum of Pericles, both of them Subjects engraved for my Second Volume. They compose admirably well, & will have in my opinion a great & a pleasing effect. We agree that this will be executed in oil, as it will then be secure from the moist effluvia of the Orange trees. The water fall, with the scenery accompanying it, he has contrived with great ingenuity. I think it will have a wonderfull effect, it must astonish & delight every spectator.[18]

The orangery was alas demolished *c.*1800 but the surviving Shepherd's Monument (Plate 13), which seems to have been in existence by 1758, is one of the most romantic of English garden buildings. A carved relief by Peter Scheemakers after Poussin's 'Et in Arcadia Ego' is sheltered by a rocky arch, the whole forming a composition so close to an engraving by Thomas Wright (Plate 14) that he is generally credited with the design of the monument.[19] However, the arch is itself fronted with a screen of two primitivist columns carrying a Doric entablature. Each of the deliberately rough-hewn drums of the columns is fluted only at the bottom, thereby suggesting a work unfinished for some mysterious reason. A drawing in Stuart's hand (Plate 15) for just such a column survives at the British Museum,[20] implying that this part of the Shepherd's Monument is an addition by Stuart.

The surviving letters from Stuart to Anson between 1764 and 1770 are a fascinating example of the curious combination of familiarity and subservience which makes it so difficult for us today to understand the precise tone of the relationship between eighteenth-century patrons and their protégés. Prompted by Stuart's work at Shugborough and 15 St James's Square, the letters are nonetheless full of details about Stuart's ill health, especially his gout, and become more familiar during the decade. In December 1764 he explained that 'I am so anxious to visit Shugborough where I persuade myself (not to mention my affections) that I have some reputation at stake, & where the blunder of a workman will torture me every time I see it, or think of it.'[21] When he died unmarried in 1772 Anson left Stuart an annuity of £100. Stuart was also in touch in the 1760s with Joseph Nollekens who was in Rome acquiring examples of antique male figure-sculpture for Anson, both originals and casts. In October 1765 Nollekens wrote to Anson, 'I have sent Mr Stuart a slite sketch of your Adonis',[22] and in the same year sent him via Stuart a cast of the antique group of the twin brothers Castor and Pollux now in the Prado. At that time Nollekens was engaged in carving the arresting marble copy of this group for Anson which is now in the Victoria and Albert Museum.

Whilst Stuart's garden buildings were rising at Shugborough he was working at Nuneham Park, Oxfordshire, for the 1st Earl Harcourt, courtier, antiquarian and founder member of the Society of Dilettanti. In *c.* 1760–4 Stuart carried out some decorative work inside the house, including a magnificent chimney-piece flanked by lion terms (Plate 16), but his chief contribution was the church of All Saints which he and Lord Harcourt designed in 1764. Nuneham Courtenay is, with Milton Abbey, Dorset, a classic instance of the eighteenth-century game of emparkment. In the 1760s Lord Harcourt demolished an entire village and parish church to make way for what was to become by the end of the following decade a classic landscape of idyllic beauty in its undulating wooded site above the Thames. Stuart's new church, which resembled a garden ornament on an unusually large scale rather than a church, was set at the end of a long newly-formed terrace walk. However, in 1777 the 2nd Lord Harcourt called on the Rev. William Mason (1724–97), painter, poet and landscape-gardener, to remodel the grounds along more pictorial lines. Mason broke up the avenue connecting the house and church so as to form a series of framed Picturesque views towards the Thames, the Berkshire downs and the towers and spires of Oxford. The result, as Horace Walpole wrote to Mason in 1782, was that 'This place is more Elysian than ever, the river full to the brim, and the church by one touch of Albano's pencil is become a temple, and a principal feature of one of the most beautiful landscapes in the world.'[23]

The architectural form of the church (Plate 17) is inspired by Palladio's Villa Rotonda near Vicenza: a porticoed square surmounted by a circular dome. However, in its elimination of all unnecessary ornament, its feeling for geometry and its impressive Greek Ionic portico, the church has a cold sobriety which points clearly to the Greek Revival of the future. At the RIBA Drawings Collection there is an attractive sketch by Stuart in pen and grey wash for a domed church with a tetrastyle Greek Doric portico (Plate 18) inspired by that in the Forum of Augustus in Athens, Greek in style but Roman in date. This is almost certainly a preliminary design for the church at Nuneham and is therefore remarkably advanced for its date. In its confident use of Greek Doric it can only be compared with Bonomi's church at Great Packington, Warwickshire, of 1789. In the church as executed, Stuart substituted the fifth-century Ionic of the Temple on the Ilissus for the sterner Greek Doric. At the same time, the church is undeniably designed for pictorial effect: its hexastyle portico on the north side contains neither door nor window but is a visual gesture designed to look well from across the park and to contain seats from which to enjoy the view.

Stuart's last recorded garden buildings are at Wimpole, Cambridgeshire, and Park Place, Berkshire. The Prospect House in the park at Wimpole Hall was erected from Stuart's designs in 1774–77 for the 2nd Earl of Hardwicke on a gentle slope to the west of the house. It was a simple Palladian building with the centre bays projecting so as to form a loggia of four Ionic columns on the ground floor and a Palladian window above. It was subsequently altered by Repton and demolished in the late nineteenth century. Like Stuart's temple at Hagley, it was conceived as a piquant balance to a ruined Gothic tower designed by Sanderson Miller. This tower was originally designed in 1750 but was not executed until 1768 under the supervision of Capability Brown who was remodelling the park in his soft generalised forms for the 2nd Earl in 1767–72. Park Place, Berkshire, laid out in the 1780s for Walpole's friend General Conway, is one of the lesser known but most romantic gardens of the later eighteenth century. The chinese house has disappeared but the surviving buildings include a rocky Cyclopic bridge of 1781–6, a grotto and a Druidic temple which is in fact an ancient stone circle brought from Jersey in 1787. There is also a long subterranean passage which 'leads to a valley bordered with cypress, containing a grand representation of a Roman amphitheatre falling into decay. The execution of this ivy-mantled ruin is of a very superior kind. The prospects are delightfully varied and extensive; and the river Thames, seen in many parts to great advantage, considerably heightens the beauty of the scene.'[24] Either the amphitheatre or a now demolished building nearby was designed by Stuart, for a contemporary account makes special mention of 'Stuart's Grecian ruins'.

3　Interior design and furniture

The transformation which the classical tradition in English architecture underwent in c. 1760 was largely one of interior decoration, layout and planning rather than of exterior forms. The Palladian palaces begun by the Whigs in the first half of the century were acceptable architecturally until at least the end of the century, but their interior design had always reflected the fashions of the day: thus the mid seventeenth-century interiors of Wilton had been French Baroque; Holkham from the 1730s had been nobly classical; Hagley in the 1750s gaily Rococo. Just as Adam's most characteristic interiors were contrived within buildings already planned or built by other architects, as at Kedleston, Osterley, Syon, Nostell and Harewood, so too were Stuart's, as at Kedleston (unexecuted), Spencer House, Wimbledon House, Nuneham and Greenwich Hospital Chapel. From the 1760s the Adam style was to hold sway. It could so easily have been the Stuart style, a new fashionably Greek style devised by the one man in Europe who knew more about Greek architecture than anyone since the ancient world. This was Adam's nightmare, the great fear that spurred on the already naturally ambitious Scot to ever greater endeavours. As it happened, Adam need not have worried. Stuart's growing preference for an 'easy and convivial life' combined with a certain lack of imaginative vitality as a creative designer, meant that he was not in the end a serious rival. But that cannot have been clear to Adam in the crucial decade from 1755–65, so that if we are to understand and enjoy the battle fought in those years we must forget for the moment our art-historical foreknowledge.

In the year of his return from Greece Stuart was employed at

31

Wentworth Woodhouse, Yorkshire, by the 2nd Marquess of Rockingham, Whig prime minister, Fellow of the Royal Society and of the Society of Antiquaries. The immense east front of what was arguably the largest country house in England, was built from designs by Flitcroft between *c.*1735 and *c.*1770. The principal interior in this wing is the vast Marble Saloon (Plate 19) adorned with niches containing copies of antique statues made for Lord Rockingham in Rome in 1749–50. Over these niches is a series of bas-relief panels designed by James Stuart in *c.*1755. These large and crisply carved reliefs in which a vase is flanked alternately by griffins and cornucopiae have all the confident emphasis of the Empire style as deployed by Percier and Fontaine in their Louvre interiors of *c.*1808. It seems that Rockingham initially intended these panels to be painted since in a letter of 28 September 1755 Stuart wrote to him, 'I will take the liberty of reminding your Lordship that the Plan of Wentworth house will be necessary to me in order to make those changes I meditate in the Back of it next the Garden, & the Connexion between it & the new hall. I likewise wish to have the size of the three Pannels in the new dining Room that I may make Sketches for the Pictures to be Painted in them, & if I had a Print of the inside of the grand Saloon I should endeavour to ornament it in the purest taste I can imagine. Mr Scott has taken measure according to your Lordship's Orders of the pannels over the doors in the Saloon of the Center house & would know if you would choose reall Views on the Thames or Pictures in which those Views are not strictly followed but something Ideal introduced...'[25]

In 1762–3 Rockingham acquired thirty-six silver and copper medals and four 'vase candlesticks' from Stuart, and in 1765 paid him £75 for purchasing and shipping from Rome a bronze lamp and an antique marble of Silenus riding a goat.

No less prestigious than his connection with Rockingham was Stuart's next commission at Kedleston, Derbyshire, where Nathaniel Curzon (created Lord Scarsdale in 1761) consulted him in *c.*1757 about the design of interiors in which to display his collection of paintings and sculpture. Robert Adam was still in Italy at this moment. The north-east wing of the great Palladian house was begun in 1759 from a general plan by Matthew Brettingham, the father of Stuart's companion in Italy, Matthew

Brettingham junior. The balancing north-west wing was carried out under the supervision of James Paine in *c.* 1760–2, but in the meantime Curzon, anxious to be as up-to-date stylistically as possible, had consulted not only Stuart but also, in December 1758, Robert Adam. Ousting both Paine and Stuart, the ambitious Adam now completed the house to a modified version of the Brettingham/Paine plans in 1760–5.

A set of drawings in Stuart's hand for the Great Saloon and possibly dining room survives in the Kedleston archives; there are also two related drawings at the RIBA. What is their significance? It has been claimed, for example, that they show that 'he was one of the first, if not the first, architect of the Neo-classical period to recognise the value of presenting to clients designs for interior decoration in which walls were shown with furniture, pictures and sculpture in place.'[26] However, William Kent (*c.*1685–1748), who worked in a variety of styles including Palladian, Baroque, neo-Classical and Gothick, prepared designs for the Saloon at Houghton Hall in *c.*1726–31 which show furniture, pictures, wall and ceiling decoration, doorcases and a chimney-piece. It would therefore be wrong to think of Stuart's idea as new, even if he presents it in a neo-Classical rather than a Baroque guise. His two-storeyed Great Saloon contained Curzon's full length sculptured figures standing on plain pedestals; between the windows were rectangular tables supporting tripod candelabra and flanked by tripod pedestals bearing busts (Plate 20). These Greek tripods, which also appeared as painted wall decoration and as incense burners on the chimney-piece, were based on Stuart's reconstruction of the metal tripod on the Choragic Monument of Lysicrates. This reconstruction was published in the first volume of the *Antiquities of Athens* to which Lord Scarsdale was a subscriber. Between the incense burners on the chimney-piece (Plate 21) Stuart shows a vase and a pair of sphinxes, while the design of the chimney-piece itself, with its lion mask and wreaths inspired by those on the Choragic Monument of Thrasyllus, pointed towards the future Greek Revival in its massiveness and antique sobriety. The room was to contain some of Scarsdale's finest Italian paintings, a number of which Stuart was intending to cut down so as to fit into his scheme of wall decoration. Above the round-headed niche at one end he planned to insert a painting by himself depicting an adventure of Bacchus inspired by the frieze on the Choragic Monument of Lysicrates (Plate 23). The balancing recess at the opposite end of the room was flanked by doorways surmounted by imitations of antique bas-reliefs. A related drawing, which may be for the dining room, shows an alcove with a sideboard sheltering a Sicilian jasper urn recently sent from Rome by the sculptor Richard Hayward (Plate 22). On either side of the sideboard was an urn standing on a pedestal adorned with addorsed griffins, imitated from a tripod now in the Capitoline Museum.

All this antique solemnity was not to be. In December 1758 Robert Adam, who was visiting the Curzons, saw Stuart's designs and wrote of them to his brother James that they were

> so excessively and ridiculously bad that Mr Curzon immediately saw the folly of them and said so to some people, which so offended the proud Grecian that he has not seen Sir Nathaniel these two years and he says he keeps the drawings sacred in self defence. He made a gallery only 5 feet high so that one would think the modern Greeks diminished in size as well as in spirit, but forgot that Brittains were taller. Then he advances his columns in his Great Hall, so much as only to leave 14 feet of space which you know was making a narrow passage of it. His ordinary Rooms beggar all description however ridiculous. I confess myself unequal to the task. Tables 2 foot sqr in a Room of 50 foot long with belts of stone and great panels and roses and festoons and figures all rammed in wherever there was a hole to be got for them and he wanted to fitt frames for Sir Nathaniel's pictures but not having or rather I suppose, not being willing to confine his great genius to the sizes of the pictures, he cutts 3 foot off the length of the best pictures and 2 foot off the height of others to make them answer and draws all the pictures and colours them in his drawings. But they move pity rather than contempt.[27]

Despite Adam's victory over Stuart, his designs for the dining room of 1762 lean heavily on Stuart's of a year or so earlier. Especially Stuartian is the tripod perfume-burner which stands on the sideboard in the alcove in Adam's dining room. At least one of these was made and survives today at Kedleston. Of exquisitely chased ormolu on a triangular marble base, it was for long attributed to Adam though it is now generally accepted as inspired by Stuart's designs. Probably made *c.* 1760 by a skilled metalworker from the Continent known as Diedrich Nicolaus Anderson, it has recently been claimed as the origin of the countless tripods or *athéniennes* which appeared in European design up to and including the Empire style in the form of 'decorative motifs in painted and plastered wall panels, as tables, as stands for vases, candelabra or statues, as perfume burners as supports for tea urns and centrepieces.'[28] However, such tripods had been a feature of French interest in the antique as early as the reign of Louis XIV. For example, the sculptor François Girardon (1628–1715) had published an engraving by 1709 (Plate 24) which included a pair of antique revival gilt-wood tripods, not dissimilar to Stuart's, made for his gallery and studio in the Louvre.

Perfume-burners were popular not only because of their antique form and vague association with what were thought to be antique Roman habits. At dinner parties in elegant households incense was burnt in them while dessert was being served so as to drive out the lingering effluvia of cooked meat. Similar tripod perfume-burners to that at Kedleston were made to Stuart's designs for Wentworth Woodhouse and for Spencer House, St James's, London. The Wentworth Woodhouse burner survives at the Victoria and Albert Museum, while a pair of more elaborate burners from Spencer House survives, along with much other important Stuart furniture, in the collection of the present Lord Spencer at Althorp, Northamptonshire. Stuart decorated a suite of rooms on the first floor of Spencer House from about 1759. His distinguished patron was John Spencer (1734–83), who was created 1st Baron and Viscount Spencer in 1761 and 1st Earl Spencer in 1765, in which year he became a member of the Society of Dilettanti. In 1756–65 this young man employed John Vardy, a disciple of William Kent, to build Spencer House. Colonel George Gray, Secretary of the Dilettanti Society, supervised the design and it was doubtless he who called in Stuart to enliven Vardy's neo-Palladianism with something more fashionably antique. The result was in many ways the most magnificent domestic interiors of eighteenth-century London, unsurpassed for the dazzling quality of the fittings and the unity of architecture, furniture and decoration. The dismantling of the interiors in the 1920s by the 7th Earl Spencer, who removed the finest chimney-pieces and doors to Althorp, was one of the major architectural tragedies of the twentieth century.

The Painted Room on the first floor, which is Stuart's finest surviving interior, represents the realisation of the themes he had developed in his unexecuted designs for Kedleston. The room is a tour de force in the ancient Roman 'Grotesque' or arabesque type of decoration which had been revived in Renaissance Italy by Raphael, Vasari, Giovanni da Udine and their followers. Fine examples survive in the Palazzo Vecchio, Florence, the Villa Madama and in the Vatican *logge* which provided the particular source for Stuart's arabesque pilaster panels. William Kent had already revived the 'Grotesque' style for two painted ceilings of the 1730s at Kensington Palace and Rousham, Oxfordshire, but not until Clérisseau's salon at the Hôtel Grimod de la Reynière in Paris of the 1770s was France to see anything comparable. Stuart subordinated the painted ornament to a strongly architectonic frame enriched with Greek motifs and fine plasterwork. However, it is the colourful exuberance of the large-scale paintings which makes the strongest visual impact on the visitor to the room, and it cannot really be claimed that their warmth, richness and gaiety produce an overall effect which one would immediately describe as neo-Classical.

The north wall of the Painted Room is divided into three bays by pilasters which correspond to the screen of Corinthian columns in front of the bow-windowed apse at the south end of the room (Plates 25, 26). This screen and its soffit is derived from the portico of the Temple of Antoninus and Faustina in Rome, while the doorcases and the mirrors in the apse have fluted friezes inspired by those in the colonnade of the Incantada at Salonica (Thessalonike). This curious building, probably of the late second century AD, was illustrated in the *Antiquities of Athens* and dismantled in the nineteenth century (Plate 27). The elaborate chimney-piece is flanked by female terms and, unusually, has a painted frieze based on the 'Aldobrandini Wedding', a celebrated ancient Roman painting in the Vatican. Above this are three bronzed plaster reliefs of amorini. The north wall, for which a drawing by Stuart dated 1759 survives in the British Museum (Plate 28), is a specially elaborate example of his skill as a painter and colourist. The ground colour, as throughout the room, is a bluish-green enlivened with much gilding. Each of the two main divisions of the wall space contains a central roundel between two rectangular panels. The upper panels and the roundels are painted canvases, the former depicting magpies and turtle-doves on vine festoons, the latter captive centaurs and amorini. The rectangular panels below them are romantic landscapes painted directly on to the wall surface. These panels are linked imaginatively to each other by graceful scrolls, arabesques, tripod altars and female figures. The ceiling is divided into nine compartments, eight of which contain paintings on canvas of female dancers or of wreaths of flowers and foliage. The central compartment is adorned with twelve grisaille roundels of the signs of the zodiac arranged to form a circle. The semi-dome of the apse is divided by ribs into five sections each containing a canvas panel painted with groups of classical figures. The rich plasterwork includes a Greek key band and arabesques, flowers and anthemion ornaments.

But this sumptuous room has not yet yielded up all its treasures. It was originally adorned with splendid and appropriate neo-antique furnishings by Stuart which survive at Althorp, and at Kenwood and the Victoria and Albert Museum: two torchères, four mirrors with carved and gilded frames, four sofas with winged lion ends and six massive arm chairs. The torchères (Plate 29), nearly seven feet high, stood between the Corinthian columns and the side walls. They are important as some of the earliest furniture decorated with painted panels in a manner developed later by Adam, Wyatt and their imitators in the Empire period. The stands are painted with Pompeiian winged figures of Victory on a maroon ground, the same colour as the background of the ceiling paintings, and are surmounted by winged griffins which, in turn, support the ormolu tripods embellished with candle sconces and a central incense burner. The only feature retained from the Baroque period is the design of the scrolled feet.

37

Scarcely less magnificent were the sofas (Plate 30), two of which were designed to stand on either side of the window opposite the chimney-piece, another two having curved backs to fit under the mirrors between the windows in the apse. This arrangement ensured that anyone entering the room would see the flanks of the four sofas consisting of winged lions. The lion motif, which was doubtless adapted by Stuart from some antique Roman throne of marble which he had seen in Italy, helps make the sofas amongst the earliest examples of neo-Classical seat furniture in Europe. Much later the use of animal parts was to be a feature of Empire style furniture as in the thrones with winged sphinxes made for the Prince Regent in 1813 by Tatham and Co. The adaptation of ceremonial marble furniture for the purposes of modern domestic furniture made from wood gave both Stuart's sofas and Regency furniture much of its monumental character.

The qualities of this room were keenly appreciated by contemporaries; Arthur Young described it as 'a phoenix' in his full account of it in 1768.[29] It was still admired in 1908 when the prolific Edwardian topographer Edwin Beresford Chancellor devoted a remarkable purple patch to it in his *The Private Palaces of London, Past and Present*: 'When we enter this apartment we seem to be stepping back two thousand years; we are no longer in a London reception-room; we are in the *tablinium* in the house of Marcus Lucretius, or in one of the remarkable painted chambers in the dwelling of Meleager; that red light in the sky is not the sun setting over the trees of the Green Park, but the afterglow of some great eruption of Vesuvius! If a door open, surely Glaucus or Diomed or the blind Nydia will appear! It is truly a room in which to dream of the past...'[30]

Adjacent to the Painted Room is the great Ballroom (Plate 31) in the centre of the west front. This was completed in 1764 with a magnificent coffered ceiling by Stuart containing three shallow saucer domes. The coffered coving is overlaid in a Baroque manner with carved vases and festoons in the angles of the room and with large circular medallions in the centre of the four main faces, supported by amorini, griffins and leopards. The exquisitely carved medallions depict Music, Hospitality, Venus, and the Three Graces. Stuart designed this room as a background for Lord Spencer's paintings which, hung on a red damask background, were provided with gilt frames carved to match the door and window surrounds. The impressive door-cases at the north and south ends of the room (Plate 32) incorporated free-standing fluted Corinthian columns and a classical frieze of the Incantada type. The same frieze appeared on the monumental chimney-piece, now in the picture gallery at Althorp, which was also adorned with an impressive figured frieze inspired by that on the Choragic Monument of Lysicrates. The great pier glasses between the windows and the console tables (Plate 33) on which they stood also survive at Althorp. With the guilloche mouldings on their stretchers, the triple fluting of their square tapered legs and their block capitals with rosettes, these tables anticipate the hallmarks of much Louis XVI furniture in France and Adam furniture in England from the 1760s onwards. However, the tables are transitional in character in that the heavy swags, the egg and dart moulding below the fluted frieze and the central mask are survivals from an earlier period: perhaps an instance of Stuart the neo-Classicist paying tribute to Vardy the Palladian.

The finial from the Choragic Monument of Lysicrates provided Stuart with the inspiration for his eye-catching lantern of ormolu with its elaborate capital of gilded wood. This lantern, now at Althorp, was designed to hang on the staircase at Spencer House as a foretaste of the classical splendours on the first floor. Other Stuart furniture from Spencer House, now at Althorp, includes candle stands (Plate 34) from the Painted Room, a pier glass and semi-circular pier table from the Music Room, an impressive circular night-cupboard (Plate 35) anticipating the first Doric pillar-boxes, a mahogany wardrobe with a prominent Vitruvian scroll band as a free-standing cornice, and a mahogany chest in the form of a cassone with satinwood inlay and ormolu mouldings (Plate 36). The chest also has a Greek key frieze and elegant feet perhaps based on the lotus-leaf porch capitals of the Tower of the Winds in Athens. Less successful is a rather confused and elaborately ornamented wardrobe (Plate 37) with a swagged frieze, corner capitals and inlaid panels. However, the dignity and authority of most of these early pieces of

Greek Revival furniture show that Stuart could work out an
alternative to the showy style of the swagged pier tables in the
state rooms at Spencer House which had echoed Le Lorrain's
'goût grec' furniture for Lalive de Jully of *c.* 1756–7. Further
evidence of the striking parallel between Stuart's style in *c.* 1759
and the contemporary 'goût grec' of designers such as Le Lorrain,
Neufforge and, a little later, Delafosse, can be found in drawings
by Stuart preserved in the Pierpont Morgan Library and in the
tripod stands (Plate 38) from the Rubens Room at Spencer
House. These stands are of gilt wood on lion paw feet with fluted
legs and frieze crowned by an emphatic Greek key band. They
have something in common with two designs by Stuart for
garlanded pedestals in the Pierpont Morgan Library (Plate 39),
though his design, in the same institution, for a chimney-piece
and overmantel (Plate 40) boasts Greek Doric columns and a
triglyph frieze which would scarcely have been found at this date
in France. Stuart may have been in touch in Rome with
the leaders of French neo-Classical taste in *c.* 1750, and on
his return through Paris may have come into contact with their
work again. It may be worth pointing out in this connection
that Le Lorrain and Neufforge had helped engrave the illustrations for Le Roy's *Les plus beaux monuments de la Grèce* of
1758.

Stuart's interiors at Spencer House were not his only commission for Lord Spencer. In *c.* 1758, possibly slightly earlier than
Spencer House, he redecorated interiors for Spencer at Wimbledon House, Surrey, which had been designed in 1732 by Lord
Pembroke and Roger Morris for Sarah, Duchess of Marl-
borough. Though the interiors were destroyed by fire in 1785 it is
clear from Stuart's surviving drawings (Plate 41) and from a
contemporary description by Horace Walpole that they were in
his early bold manner characterised by emphatic roundels and
urns and also by the careful architectural placing of furniture,
chimney-pieces and specially framed paintings. Walpole
described 'A closet, ornamented and painted by Mr Stewart. the
ornaments in a good antique taste. a Hymen, the Allegro &
Penseroso, on the ceiling & in compartments, villainously
painted.'[31] Robert Adam was far more critical of Stuart's work
for Lord Spencer. Having ousted Stuart from Kedleston he was

obviously hoping to do the same at Spencer House. He therefore put it about that the interiors at Spencer House were 'pity-fulissimo', claiming that the ceilings might be 'Greek to the teeth but by God they are not handsome', and referring to Stuart contemptuously as the 'Archipelagan Architect'.[32] In public he adopted a far more generous tone, even going so far as to claim in the Preface to *The Works in Architecture of Robert and James Adam* (vol. I, 1773), that 'Mr. Stuart, with his usual elegance and taste has contributed towards introducing the true style of antique decoration.' Certainly the similarity of their decorative work and furniture design in the 1760s is evident. Indeed the superb mahogany organ-case (Plate 42) in the hall at Newby, Yorkshire, long believed to have been designed by Adam, has recently been attributed by John Cornforth[33] to Stuart. He points as evidence to a meeting in 1767 between Stuart and the squire of Newby, the collector and connoisseur William Weddell, and to a design by Stuart at the RIBA for a chimney-piece in which pairs of pilasters are flanked by free-standing Ionic columns as on the Newby organ (Plate 43). The strikingly architectural character of the organ, as well as its Greek key band and elegant tripods, is also Stuartian in flavour. The triumphal arch motif on its upper half has affinities with the Arch of Hadrian in Athens and with the plates illustrating an archway in Wood's *Ruins of Palmyra* (1753), and more particularly with Stuart's screens at Holder-nesse House and Montagu House. However, the shell-fluted apse and flanking medallions are extremely close in form to Adam's fishing house at Kedleston of *c.* 1770. Nor should it be forgotten that a handsome organ case had been built to Adam's designs in the Music Room at Kedleston as early as 1765 and that he made numerous unexecuted designs for more elaborate organs later in his career.

For whatever reasons, and we must surely include Adam's campaign against him, Stuart received few commissions in the 1760s comparable to Spencer House. From now on his style seems to move away from a Franco-Greek massiveness towards a more Adamesque manner enlivened with Greek and other antique motifs. His most important commissions of the 1760s were Holdernesse (later Londonderry) House and Lichfield House, no. 15 St James's Square. Holdernesse House, on the corner of Park Lane and Hertford Street, was decorated and perhaps designed by Stuart in *c.* 1760–5 for the 4th Earl of Holdernesse. A cultivated patron of the arts, Lord Holdernesse belonged to the Society of Dilettanti whose members frequently gathered for convivial evenings at Holdernesse House. The house, which was demolished in 1964, was substantially re-modelled by Benjamin Dean Wyatt in 1825–8. However, Wyatt preserved Stuart's splendid ceilings in the two drawing rooms on the Park Lane front and in the boudoir on the Hertford Street front. The ceiling in the north drawing room had a deep cove painted with trophies of vases in scrollwork; an Adamesque central compartment contained eight roundels surrounding a fan-shaped centre-piece (Plate 44). In the adjacent centre draw-ing room the heavily compartmented ceiling was dominated by a central octagon filled with octagonal coffering and rosettes, a motif inspired by plates in Wood's *Palmyra* (Plate 45). The rectangular and hexagonal compartments round the edge of the octagon contained paintings of flowers and exotic birds. The disposition of the whole ceiling was virtually identical to a ceiling by Stuart which survives at 15 St James's Square. In the small boudoir at Holdernesse House the ceiling was dominated by a deep cove of square coffering contrasting with delicate Pompeiian arabesques in blue, pink and green (Plate 46). Stuart provided a similar ceiling in the morning room of the now demolished Montagu House in Portman Square. The boudoir was one of a number of rooms at Holdernesse House with decorative details recorded in 1766 by the 18-year-old John Carter (Plates 47–50), an architect better known for his draw-ings of medieval antiquities. Carter had an eye for novel neo-Classical ornament and many of the pen and ink wash drawings in his book record Adam's early work at Bowood, Syon, and Coventry House, Piccadilly. We know that Adam himself was not above copying a Stuart detail, for one of his drawings preserved at Sir John Soane's Museum[34] is of an entablature with egg and dart moulding in the dressing room at Spencer House.

Whilst work was in progress at Holdernesse House Stuart received a commission for another London mansion from Thomas Anson, his patron at Shugborough. 15 St James's Square rose from Stuart's designs in 1764–6 and is the only surviving example of a domestic facade by him. The first stone-fronted facade in the otherwise brick-built square, it has an air of reticent authority and refined scholarship which is partly produced by its immaculate Erectheion Ionic order (Plate 51). Fundamentally it is a Palladian composition like Spencer House in which an engaged and pedimented order stands on a rusticated ground floor with round-arched openings. The satisfying compactness of Stuart's neat three-bay composition inspired Adam's similar facade of 1771–5 at 20 St James's Square. The design and execution of the four Greek Ionic capitals took up a good deal of Stuart's time in 1764. Indeed, the frequency with which he wrote to Anson of their progress reveals him once more as a designer more interested in ornamental details than in architecture in the round. In the autumn of 1764 he explained that 'the Capitals, concerning which I do for the honour of Athens interest myself very much, are not yet finished, your house is a topic of much conversation among the connoisseurs in Architecture.' Later he confessed that 'I shall not know how to quit London till I see a Capital compleated. Scheemaker has taken two of the Volutes into his Care but my inspection & instruction is continually necessary till one of them is finished, they must not murder my Capitals the greatest grace & ornament of the building'; in October he congratulated himself on the fact that 'I knew that they would be nearly the same size with the originals but was not aware that there is not a hairs breath of difference in their Diameters.'[35] Though the dimensions of Stuart's capitals may well be identical to those of the Erectheion, the far greater simplicity of his architrave and frieze helps render idle any serious comparison between the two buildings.

The rarely seen south or courtyard elevation of 15 St James's Square is adorned with four pairs of Doric pilasters flanking a central round-arched opening so as to form the Venetian window motif. This is inspired by the Ionic frontispiece to the Aqueduct of Hadrian as illustrated in volume three of the *Antiquities of Athens*. From that monument Stuart also borrowed the springing of the arch direct from the architrave and not from the cymatium of the cornice, so that the arch thus cuts into the entablature. He defended this apparent irregularity by arguing that an arch ought to spring from a more solid base than a cymatium which represents a gutter. Similar Romano-Greek sources can be found for many of the decorative features of the interior: the curved fluted frieze of the Incantada at Salonica inspired the architraves to the doors and windows in the first-floor drawing room (Plate 52); the chimney-piece in the same room has a figured frieze inspired by that of the Choragic Monument of Lysicrates (Plate 53), and the octagonally coffered ceiling is a Palmyrene type. In the outer compartments of the ceiling are eight painted panels of classical figure-subjects by Biagio Rebecca. The rear first-floor drawing room has an Adamesque ceiling with a fan-shaped centre-piece and a cove decorated with rinceaux and defined by bands of Greek key pattern. The semi-circular bowed end was added to this room by Samuel Wyatt who remodelled or completed the interiors of the house in 1791–4. He worked in an Adamesque style close to Stuart's so that it is not always easy to disentangle their contributions.

The novelty and distinction of Stuart's facade at 15 St James's Square, which came to be known as Lichfield House, were admired by John Stewart in a lively pamphlet published anonymously in 1771 under the title *Critical Observations on the Buildings and Improvements of London*. Indeed, partly on account of its praise of Lichfield House, the pamphlet has long been erroneously attributed to James Stuart. Its author criticises the blankness of facades such as that of Norfolk House in St James's Square, built from designs by Brettingham in 1728–32, complaining that '"All the blood of all the Howards" can never ennoble Norfolk House.'[36] Arguing that 'the front to the street should still present something that intimates a relation to the society in which you live', he drew favourable attention in this respect to Stuart's 15 St James's Square: 'When once this last is completed according to the plan, the public will be able to do justice to the classic taste which directed it. In its present state it is wonderfully beautiful, and will serve to convey the idea of what is here meant.'[37] The only other recent London houses admired by John Stewart are the still surviving pair built in *c.*1770 as a commercial speculation on the north side of Cavendish Square by George Tufnell, MP. These impressive columnar mansions occupy the site owned from 1743–56 by the Society of Dilettanti who were proposing to erect on it a handsome clubhouse. In 1751 they commissioned designs from Vardy but two years later decided to base the facade on the temple at Pola recently measured by Stuart and Revett. In July 1752, by which time a quantity of Portland stone had already arrived on the site, Sir Francis Dashwood wrote to Colonel Gray in connection with this project: 'My model is advanced as far as the Capitals, and my rascally french architect is ran off and has left nothing but his debts... When the model will be finished I cannot now take upon me to say.'[38] The scheme was abandoned in 1756 but the stylistic closeness of Tufnell's houses to the park front of Spencer House, together with a degree of architectural display incongruous for domestic purposes, leads one to speculate whether they do not incorporate some cut stone prepared for the clubhouse on Vardy's directions.

Stuart's interiors at 15 St James's Square, elegant though they are, lack something of the panache of those at Spencer House. It seems that he could not develop his early sculpturesque and painterly style into a coherent and recognisably individual manner. It is no longer possible for us to trace the development of his career, after Anson's house, as though it were a measured logical process. From now on his commissions are random, his life one of cheerful indolence, and his works often completed by other hands.

4 Late works

The only works of importance by Stuart that remain to be discussed are the product of his leisurely days in the 1770s and 80s: two houses (both now demolished) begun in c. 1775 for Sir Sampson Gideon and Mrs Montagu, and the interiors at Greenwich Hospital Chapel of 1780–88 which are partly the work of William Newton. Montagu House, 22 Portman Square, was built in c. 1775–82 for Mrs Elizabeth Montagu (1720–1800), the leading hostess in fashionable literary London. In the 1760s she had employed Robert Adam to carry out extensive alterations at her house in Hill Street, Mayfair, so her decision to employ his rival, 'Athenian' Stuart, was as unusual as it must have been gratifying to Stuart. Describing her dressing room in a letter to her sister in January 1767, she explained that 'Mr Adam has done his best, he has exerted much genius on the doors in emulation of his rival Stewart.'[39] She had originally intended to employ Adam for Montagu House, 'but the great man kept her waiting an hour and brought a regiment of talking artificers.'[40] She subsequently affirmed: 'I chose him [Stuart] for my architect on account of his disinterestedness & contempt of money.'[41] She must have had reason to regret her choice when she saw the speed with which Adam completed Home House, 20 Portman Square, just a few yards away from her own slowly-rising house. One of the finest town houses of Adam's career, Home House was built and furnished in 1774–6 for Mrs Montagu's great social rival, Elizabeth, Countess of Home, the daughter of a Jamaican merchant. The perfect unity of design and decoration at Home House, culminating in two masterly interiors, the music room and circular domed staircase, represents a peak of artistic achievement which Stuart, it must be confessed, could not attain.

Stuart had corresponded with Mrs Montagu as early as July 1759 about painting a scene from *The Tempest*,[42] and in 1767 painted her bedroom at Sandleford Priory with 'some of the sweetest Zephyrs and Zephirettes'.[43] She later employed James Wyatt to remodel Sandleford as one of the earliest Gothic Revival country houses in England. For thirty years from 1750 she held a dazzling salon in Hill Street for the leading intellects of the day such as Burke, Johnson, Walpole, Reynolds, Garrick, and Lord Lyttelton who may have introduced her to Stuart. In February 1761 we find Stuart writing her a long mock-heroic letter, perhaps in the hope of soliciting architectural commissions: 'A Load of Treasure is at Athens', he explained; 'I offer my shoulders to the Shafts, as if I were a Cart-Horse: & regardless of fatigue & danger, resolve to dragg it, where alass tis greatly wanted; even to this fair flourishing Isle. Oh – toilsome task – Ah, tedious way! how slow I move – what obstacles I meet! – from Athens to London, no road has yett been made for such conveyance.'[44]

Following the death in 1775 of her husband, who left her an income of £7,000 a year, she commissioned Stuart to design her a free-standing mansion in the newly laid out Portman Square (Plate 54). It is not known whether the extremely novel site of the house, placed diagonally across the north-west corner of the square, was her idea or Stuart's. It was imitated much later when the corner mansions were built in Belgrave Square from 1826–42. The relation of Montagu House to Portman Square was undeniably more arresting than the composition of its facades. The three-storeyed seven-bay entrance front was largely unadorned save for a Venetian window at each end with details inspired by the Aqueduct of Hadrian. Inside, the planning (Plates 55, 56) of both the ground and first floors was graceless and confused, lacking the architectural coherence and spatial organisation for which Adam was already becoming known and which Stuart echoed in a sectional drawing (Plate 57), surviving at the RIBA, for a Pantheon-like villa with a rotunda and portico.

The chaste entrance hall (Plate 58) at Montagu House with its screen of free-standing Ionic columns led into the spacious top-lit staircase with a wrought-iron balustrade identical to that in Stuart's now demolished Belvedere, Kent. Montagu House, which was ready for occupation by March 1781, was visited and admired in the following February by Horace Walpole who wrote to William Mason: 'I dined on Monday with the Harcourts at Mrs Montagu's new palace, and was much surprised. Instead of vagaries it is a noble simple edifice ... though I had thought it so magnificent a house there was not a morsel of gilding, it is grand not tawdry, nor larded and embroidered and pomponned with shreds and remnants and *clinquant* like all the harlequinades of Adam, which never let the eye repose a moment.'[45]

Further decorative work, including gilding, was carried out in the 1780s and 90s so that the house was in the end richer than when Walpole first saw it. Nonetheless, Walpole's testimony shows that it was possible to believe that Stuart had invented a noble and austere alternative to the Adam style. James 'Hermes' Harris, a friend of Mrs Montagu, was similarly enraptured with her new house, exclaiming after his visit, 'I have seen an Edifice which for the time made me imagine I was at Athens, in a House of Pericles, built by Phidias.'[46] Harris was a well-known philosopher, two of whose books were adorned with illustrated frontispieces designed by Stuart. We know that the house attracted considerable attention since Mrs Montagu wrote to her agent on 26 April 1780: 'It appears to be very necessary that no one sh^d be admitted to see our House without tickets, & you will be so good as to give them to whomsoever you please ... It mortifies me to be obliged to exclude any one who wishes to see the House, as such exclusions disoblige, but one cannot allow the painting &c to be damaged. I should be glad that Valency only shew'd the House to those who have tickets.'[47]

The most elaborately decorated ground-floor room was the Morning Room (Plate 59) with a white and gold coffered cove ornamented with scroll-work in the corners: again, a type which recurs at Belvedere and Holdernesse House. The elaborate ceiling is a familiar Adam pattern of intersecting circles. Adam is again called to mind in the Reception Room upstairs (Plate 60). With its apsed ends with semi-domes and its segmental vault, this beautiful apartment is a response to Adam's second drawing room at 20 St James's Square (1771–5), one of the most highly decorated state apartments in Georgian London. The ceiling in Stuart's room was decorated by Angelica Kauffmann (1741–1807), while another of Adam's leading decorative painters Biagio Rebecca (1735–1808) provided the painted overdoors of Shakespearean themes. Mrs Montagu employed her relative by marriage Matthew Boulton, the celebrated Birmingham metalworker, to advise on the interior decoration of her new house. He in turn called on the architect James Wyatt in 1776 whom he instructed to take advice from Rebecca and G. B. Cipriani (1727–85). Further work by this distinguished collaboration could be seen on the first floor in the drawing room (Plate 61) and adjacent small drawing room. A screen of two free-standing Siena-marble scagliola columns of the Erectheion Ionic order, complete with corresponding pilasters, supported a round-headed coffered arch separating the two drawing rooms. This handsome motif was echoed at Holdernesse House, according to one of John Carter's drawings at the Victoria and Albert Museum (Plate 48), while the fluted frieze was inspired by Stuart's favourite Incantada at Salonica. The small drawing room, which boasted a segmentally vaulted ceiling painted in the Pompeiian style, contained pilasters and semi-circular overdoors in the grotesque or arabesque style recalling Stuart's Painted Room at Spencer House.

The most remarkable room at Montagu House was the elliptically vaulted Ballroom (Plate 62) which ran from the front to the back of the house at the north-east end of the first floor. In this magnificently painted apartment the door and window surrounds were, somewhat unusually, of white marble, while the whole space was defined by green scagliola columns and piers with gilded Corinthian capitals. The elaborately compartmented ceiling with its paintings of Olympus, its long figured friezes in imitation of antique bas-reliefs and its bands of intertwining laurel leaves, was one of the tours de force of eighteenth-century English neo-Classicism. In general form it may have been inspired by Adam's barrel-vaulted library at Kenwood, though it is more Graeco-Roman than Adamesque in mood. In fact, it seems not to have been executed until after Stuart's death for he had obviously become an impossible person with whom to do business by the late 1770s. The decoration of the room was thus finally carried out on the basis of a design which Joseph Bonomi

(1739–1808) exhibited at the Royal Academy in 1790 (Plate 63). This drawing survives, together with a number of others in Bonomi's hand for interiors at Montagu House, and there can be little doubt that most of the decorative and architectural features which they contain are realisations of Stuart's original intentions. Certainly they do not resemble surviving interiors by Bonomi at Packington Hall and church, Longford Hall, Laverstoke Park and Hatchlands.

In the letter to her agent of April 1780, from which we have already quoted, Mrs Montagu enlarged on the failings in Stuart's character and professional conduct which eventually led to the completion of her house by other hands:

> ... what workmen did by bribery of guineas to many architects, could be effected on him by pipes & tobacco & pots of Porter in ale houses & night Cellars. I speak it not on suspicion but certain information that since he began my House he has been for a fortnight together in the most drunken condition with these fellows [i.e. the workmen]. Mr Sampson Gideon, for whom he was building a House when I began mine, was obliged to take many precautions to prevent being imposed on by the workmen whose bills he assented to. about a year & half ago Stuart had by a long uninterrupted state of drunkenness brought himself into such a condition of mind & body as I feared irrecoverable. to this I attribute the many falsehoods of which I gave him proof by shewing to him his own letters. Tho he does not mean (I believe) to tell fibs, it is impossible to rely on any thing he says. It w^d be tedious to tell you how often I have been obliged to confront him with the workmen whom he blamed for not having executed his orders, & he was then obliged to confess he had forgotten to deliver the designs... In business the strait line is the line of beauty, but Stuart is apt to chuse the waving line.

Montagu House (or Portman House as it was known from 1874 when it became the town house of its ground landlord Viscount Portman), was gutted by an incendiary bomb in the early years of the Second World War. Though the exterior was largely intact, it was not restored and rebuilt after the war, as it would have been in almost any other European capital, and tragically there is no proper record of it apart from a set of eight photographs taken by Bedford Lemere in 1894. Equally unfortunately, no proper visual record was made when Stuart's Belvedere (Plate 64) near Erith in Kent was demolished as recently as 1960, so that the details of its complex building history are likely to remain uncertain.

Belvedere was a substantial early Georgian mansion commanding 'a vast extent of a fine country many miles beyond the Thames ... as pleasing a landskip of the kind as imagination can form.'[48] Additions were made in the 1750s by Sampson Gideon, a rich Portuguese Jew from Stepney, for whose son, Sir Sampson Gideon, Bt (1745–1824), Stuart completely rebuilt it *c.* 1775–6, reorientating it in the process. By a spectacular process of graft Sir Sampson was created a baronet at the age of thirteen through the influence of his father and was elevated to the Irish Peerage as Baron Eardley in 1789. He was elected to the Society of Dilettanti in 1767 and was Tory MP for Cambridge from 1770–80.

With its Diocletian windows and canted bays in the villa style of Ware, Paine, or Carr of York, Belvedere recalled Stuart's Montagu House. The centre of the rear facade was a striking composition with a Venetian window (Plate 65) approached by a two-armed staircase and surmounted by a huge semi-circular window with radiating glazing bars à la Adam. Some of the interiors were, as we have noted, close to Montagu House. The spectacular dining room contained thirteen inset paintings by Angelica Kauffmann and a chimney-piece flanked by fluted columns of the Erectheion Ionic order. In another room there were wall, door and chimney-piece decorations of die-stamped pewter supplied by Matthew Boulton, friend and sometime collaborator of Stuart. Elsewhere, a superb chimney-piece, now in Charleston, South Carolina, was adorned with Wedgwood plaques of green and lilac jasper depicting Venus, Cupid and swans based on designs by Le Brun (Plates 66, 67). Probably supplied in the later 1780s, this chimney-piece is of richly but finely carved pine-wood and is stylistically close to the interiors at Greenwich Hospital Chapel.

Stuart's dilatoriness, which may have led to the completion of Montagu House in the 1790s by Bonomi and the decorator P. M. Borgnis, caused even greater problems at Greenwich Hospital Chapel. In 1779 a great part of Queen Mary's buildings, including the chapel, was gutted and largely destroyed by fire. Stuart, who had occupied the sinecure post of Surveyor of Greenwich Hospital since 1758, was therefore called on to repair the damage. The architect Robert Mylne (1733–1811), then better known as a structural engineer, had been Clerk of the Works at Greenwich since 1775. Stuart, naturally lazy and no longer in good health, left most of the work to Mylne. The roof and interior of the gutted chapel had been erected in the 1730s from designs by Thomas Ripley. Rebuilding began in the summer of 1781 but Mylne soon complained to the Board of Governors of Stuart's inadequacies, including his failure to produce drawings. Stuart in turn complained that Mylne was trying to substitute drawings by himself. In September 1782 the Board replaced Mylne with William Newton (1735–90) who had been working as Stuart's assistant since the previous February. Newton, an exceptionally talented draughtsman who designed in an elegant Adam style, was also the author of the first English translation of Vitruvius in 1771. In 1787 he helped edit and complete the second volume of Stuart and Revett's *Antiquities of Athens*.

In an expanded version of his edition of Vitruvius, published in 1791 a year after his death, Newton claimed of the Greenwich Hospital Chapel (Plate 68) that 'the only parts of the building in which Mr Stuart had any share were the ornaments of the ceiling, the frame of the altar picture and the balusters used in the two side galleries; these with the carvings of some stone mouldings, taken from Greek examples in his *Antiquities of Athens*, were all that he determined; the remainder were of my designing, or my selecting, where the antique has been selected.'[49] The boldness and specificity of this claim mean that it must be taken very seriously. It is certainly borne out by the presence of over 120 working drawings for the chapel and its decoration in Newton's hand which survive in the RIBA Drawings Collection. It thus seems clear that though the general character and form of this brilliant interior were established by Stuart its realisation and the design of its parts were left to Newton. The delectable carved foliage on the galleries and their supports, on the ceiling, organ loft and doorcases, has a rich succulence which goes beyond fifth-century Athens in the direction of a Hellenistic or even Palmyrene freedom (Plate 69). There is nonetheless a certain crispness and stiffness about the details which seem characteristically Stuartian and recognisably different from the fluidity of Adam. Perhaps its origin may partly be found in the process of turning measured drawings into engravings for the meticulous plates of the *Antiquities of Athens.*

The organ screen at the west end is the most memorable feature of the interior. In the first design (Plate 70), the white marble columns have lotus-leaf capitals inspired by those on the Tower of the Winds in Athens. It thus resembled the baldacchino in Newton's unexecuted designs of 1774–5 for St Mary's, Battersea. However, in the Greenwich screen as executed (Plate 71), the order was changed to the richer and more delicate Erectheion Ionic, presumably at Stuart's suggestion (Plates 72–74). At the east end the exquisite lotus and palmette frieze which surrounds Benjamin West's altar piece of 1780, was designed by Stuart on the model of the necking band of the Erectheion Ionic order. Again, this was a substitute for a clumsier coffered design by Newton. In the spandrels above are angels carved in 1785 by John Bacon, RA (1740–99) at Newton's request but without Stuart's express approval. Bacon also made designs for a pediment and carved the frieze of the doorcase in 1789. Other marble work was executed in 1788 at a cost of £1,897 by the mason-contractor and sculptor John Deval, junior (1728–94). Painters of similar quality were employed to adorn the upper walls of the chapel. Between the windows a series of sixteen monochrome roundels depicting New Testament scenes were painted in oil on canvas in *c.* 1779 by Rebecca, Milbourne, Theodore de Bruyn and Charles Catton. Rebecca also provided the monochrome overdoors in the gallery portraying four prophets based on designs by Benjamin West.

Especially eye-catching is the circular pulpit (Plate 75) inspired by the Choragic Monument of Lysicrates. In view of Stuart's known fondness for this Hellenistic monument as exemplified in aspects of his designs for Shugborough, Spencer House and

Kedleston, it seems reasonable to attribute to him this unique adoption of its form for the purposes of a pulpit.[50] The details, however, were worked out by Newton as is clear from the surviving drawings. The result is one of the most remarkable and stylish pieces of English eighteenth-century furniture. Constructed of oak and mahogany by the joiners Lawrence and Arrow, it is ringed with six columns with exquisitely carved Corinthian capitals of the Lysicratean order supporting a frieze based on a plate in *The Antiquities of Ionia*, published in 1769 by Revett, Chandler and Pars. In place of the pagan frieze of the Choragic Monument is a series of Coade stone medallions designed by Benjamin West depicting scenes from the life of St Paul. Also of Coade stone are the six cherubim which delightfully support the novel semi-oval altar. Designs for this survive in Newton's hand. The chapel was finished by Newton after Stuart's death in 1788 (Plates 76–77) when, in pursuance of his claim that he was the real architect of the building, Newton appealed unsuccessfully to the governors for professional remuneration in addition to his salary as Clerk of the Works.

As well as his work as an architect and designer of furniture and interior decoration, Stuart was involved from the first with the design of medals (Plate 78) based on Roman prototypes, with silverware and with about half a dozen funerary monuments – fields in which his gift for elegant small-scale ornament was very appropriately deployed. In 1757 he designed the first medal issued by the Royal Society of Arts and at about this time designed a series of medals which were struck to commemorate the victories of the Seven Years' War. These were used as a source for some of the elegant plaster medallions added to the Temple of Concord and Victory at Stowe in the 1750s; indeed it seems that Earl Temple devised this scheme of decoration on advice from Stuart. Stuart was also associated with the great manufacturer Matthew Boulton with whom he was in correspondence as early as 1769 about providing a 'tripodic Tea-Kitchen'[51] for Shugborough. In 1771 and again in 1781 he and Boulton were associated in the design and manufacture of two handsome silver soup tureens for the Admiralty.[52] These were in the chaste Louis XVI style which he also used for his funerary monuments, enlivened with conventional putti, swags, urns, sarcophagi and obelisks. One of the finest of these monuments, which were mostly executed by Thomas or Peter Scheemakers, was that in the church at Wimpole, Cambridgeshire, to the 1st Earl of Hardwicke (died 1764) and his wife (Plate 79). Stuart wrote enthusiastically about this commission to his friend Thomas Anson and explained that 'Skeemakers is resolved to make it his masterpiece, he is hugely pleased with it.' In September 1764 Stuart sent Anson a drawing of the monument and a description of its iconography:

> on one side is Minerva, not the Warlike but the Eloquent & therefore instead of the Lance, she holds a Caduceus, for this I have authority. On the other side is Pudicitia, the matronal Virtue. She is veild & holds a stem of Lilies. One Sarcophagus is supposed to hold them both, & the Medallions on the Sarcophagus are their Portraits in Profile.
>
> On the Stereobata are four Children, of the two middle-most, one collects the Mace and Purse &c. the other crowns it with a Garland. on the side of Minerva is a Boy who is composing other Crowns, & on the side of Pudicitia is a Boy who gives a stem of Lilies to him who collects the decorations of Office.[53]

One maverick commission which ought to be recorded is Stuart's only known Gothic design. This was in 1771 for the east window, altar and reredos at St George's Chapel, Windsor (Plate 80). It is an uninformed Gothic design in which the grey-coloured reredos was completely overwhelmed by a vast painted circular window containing coats of arms centred on a Garter badge enclosing the royal arms. Characteristically where Stuart was concerned, we find the Dean and Chapter complaining to him in 1771 that unless his design was submitted by midsummer the commission would be given to another architect. However, they paid him in July though the executed design, presumably also by Stuart, was not Gothic but classical. In 1785–6 this work was removed, largely on the king's orders, on the grounds that it was 'of Grecian architecture, & not of course corresponding with the stile of the Chapel.'[54] It was replaced with a design by Sandby, executed and slightly altered by Henry Emlyn (*c.* 1729–1815), an expert Gothicist who provided numerous convincingly Perpendicular fittings elsewhere in the chapel.[55]

By the 1780s, according to J. T. Smith in *Nollekens and his Times*, Stuart 'regularly frequented a public-house on the north side of Leicester-fields, of the sign of the Feathers.' He also wrote of him that 'Mr. Stuart, though short, was not a fat, but rather a heavy-looking, man, and his face declared him to be fond of what is called friendly society.'[56] Stuart was twice married, on the first occasion to a person variously reported as his housekeeper[57] and as a 'Grecian lady',[58] and on the second, at the age of sixty-seven, to a girl of twenty by whom he had five children. He died suddenly at his house on the south side of Leicester Square on 2 February 1788 and was buried in the crypt of St Martin in the Fields. 'Unexpectedly to most people ... [he was] possessed of much property, chiefly on mortgage on new buildings in Marylebone.'[59] In the preface to the second volume of *The Antiquities of Athens*, William Newton explained that 'Mr. Stuart, having been very infirm for some years preceding his death, left his papers in great confusion and disorder; many were incomplete, and several were missing.'[60] Stuart's choice of executor was, characteristically, a man of dissipated habits who 'died of maddness in a London Workhouse'.[61] The consequent loss of his personal papers has made the task confronting his modern biographers a frustrating one. A pathetic souvenir of Stuart survives at Sir John Soane's Museum in the form of his now empty paint-box, acquired by Soane and inscribed by him, 'Formerly belonged to poor Stuart', a phrase suggesting affectionate regret at a life of lost opportunities.

Finally, a word should perhaps be said at this stage about Stuart's friend and partner Nicholas Revett. After he had sold his interest in the *Antiquities of Athens* to Stuart, he joined Chandler and Pars on their expedition to the coast of Asia Minor in 1764–66. He prepared the measured drawings of the antiquities and subsequently prepared them for publication by the Dilettanti Society as *The Antiquities of Ionia* (2 vols., 1769–97). Being possessed of private means he worked for clients even less than Stuart. His alterations at Standlynch (now Trafalgar House), Wiltshire (*c.* 1766) and at West Wycombe Park, Buckinghamshire (1771–80), and his church at Ayot St Lawrence, Hertford-

shire (1778), are interesting but minor monuments in the history
of the Greek Revival. Their significance is less in what they are
than in who designed them.

Despite Stuart's undoubted role as a pioneer if patchy Greek
Revivalist, it may at the same time be helpful to remember that
his achievement, like that of Adam and Wyatt, was facilitated by
the importation of Italian artists, craftsmen and decorators.
These men were expert in the creation of interiors enlivened with
painted decoration and plasterwork based on classical models: a
tradition which went back in Italy to the golden years of the
Renaissance in the fifteenth and sixteenth centuries. Moreover,
Kent, Stuart, Chambers, Adam, Mylne, Dance, Wyatt and Soane
all spent formative years in Rome. Perhaps we should consider
their work for a moment as simply a late stage in the acclimatisa-
tion of England to the ideals of the Italian Renaissance.

Notes

1 British Library, Add. MSS 27576, f. 50.
2 *Civil Engineer and Architect's Journal*, X, 1847, pp. 338–9.
3 D. Wiebenson, *Sources of Greek Revival Architecture*, 1969, p. 76.
4 *Ibid.*, pp. 77–8.
5 Society of Dilettanti, MSS Minutes, vol. II, 1745–60, 3 March 1751, Stuart and Revett proposed by Sir J. Gray and elected. 'A Motion made and agreed to that the Society do subscribe as a Body to the Proposals of Mr Stewart & Rivett.' In March 1757 it was resolved to 'present the authors of the Antiquities of Attica with the sum of Twenty Guineas for their first Volume, and for the further encouragement of so great and useful a work to intend the same sum for each Volume as they shall be published.'
6 *Antiquities of Athens*, IV, 1816, p. iv.
7 T. J. Mulvany, *The Life of James Gandon*, 1846, p. 199.
8 J. Paine, *Plans, Elevations and Sections*, I, 1767, p. ii.
9 L. Lawrence, 'Stuart and Revett', *Jnl. of the Warburg Inst.*, II, 1938–9, pp. 136–7.
10 *Complete Works of Sir J. Vanbrugh*, IV, The Letters (ed. G. Webb, 1928), p. 30.
11 R. Blunt, ed., *Mrs Montagu, 'Queen of the Blues'*, 1923, II, p. 150.
12 C. Hussey, *English Country Houses, Early Georgian 1715–60*, rev. ed. 1965, p. 200.
13 L. Dickins & M. Stanton ed., *An Eighteenth-century Correspondence*, 1910, p. 297.
14 Stuart to Anson, 17 June 1796 (Staffordshire Record Office, Anson MSS).
15 Stuart to Anson, 23 September 1769 (Staffordshire Record Office, Anson MSS).
16 Stuart to Anson, 19 June 1764 (Staffordshire Record Office, Anson MSS).
17 Lady Anson to T. Anson, 24 May 1760 (Staffordshire Record Office, Anson MSS): 'Mr Stewart desires to be informed of the *number & size* of your Dorick columns; having made the Drawing of your Portico, which he wants to make the Scale to before he sends it.'
18 Stuart to Anson, 25 September 1770 (Staffordshire Record Office, Anson MSS).
19 T. Wright, *Arbours and Grottos* (E. Harris ed., 1979), pp. 35–6.
20 British Library, Add. MSS 22153, f. 177.
21 Stuart to Anson, 19 December 1764 (Staffordshire Record Office, Anson MSS).
22 Nollekens to Anson, 30 October 1765 (Staffordshire Record Office, Anson MSS).

23 Horace Walpole to William Mason, 13 October 1782 (Walpole, *Correspondence*, ed. W. S. Lewis, XXIX, 1955, p. 85); and see M. L. Batey, 'William Mason, Gardener', *Garden History*, I, no. 2, Feb. 1973, pp. 11–25).

24 *Patersons Roads*, 16th ed., 1822, I, p. 114.

25 Stuart to Rockingham, 28 September 1755 (Sheffield Central Library, Rockingham Papers, R1/70).

26 J. Harris, *Architectural History*, XXII, 1979, p. 72.

27 J. Hardy and H. Hayward, 'Kedleston Hall, Derbyshire – II', *Country Life*, 2 February 1978, p. 263.

28 N. Goodison, 'Mr Stuart's Tripod', *Burlington Magazine*, CXIV, 1972, p. 704; and S. Erikson and F. Watson, 'The "Athénienne" and the Revival of the Classical Tripod', *ibid.*, CV, 1963, pp. 108–12. I am indebted to Dr Robin Middleton for drawing my attention to Girardon's tripods, on which see F.Souchal, 'La collection du sculpteur Girardon', *Gazette des Beaux-Arts*, LXXXII, July–August 1973, pl. II and p. 88.

29 A. Young, *A Six Weeks Tour*, 2nd ed., 1769, pp. 359–60.

30 E. B. Chancellor, *The Private Palaces of London*, 1908, p. 342.

31 H. Walpole, 'Visits to Country Seats', *Walpole Society*, XVI, p. 15.

32 J. Fleming, *Robert Adam and his Circle*, 1962, p. 258.

33 J. Cornforth, 'Newby Hall, Yorkshire – I', *Country Life*, 7 June 1979, p. 1806.

34 Sir John Soane's Museum, Adam Drawings, Vol. LIV, 3rd series, no. 40, inscribed 'For the Dressing Rooms of Mr. Spencer's House by Mr. S'.

35 Stuart to Anson, September, 6 October and November 1764 (Staffordshire Record Office, Anson MSS).

36 [J. Stewart], *Critical Observations*, 1771, p. 28.

37 *Ibid.*, p. 32.

38 Sir Francis Dashwood to Colonel Gray, 19 July 1753 (Society of Dilettanti MSS I, 1736–1800, f. 105).

39 Blunt, *op.cit.*, I, p. 53.

40 *Ibid.*, II, p. 13.

41 Mrs Montagu to Leonard Smelt, 26 April 1789 (Huntington Library, MO 50256).

42 Stuart to Mrs Montagu, 14 July 1759 (Huntington Library MO 5135).

43 Blunt, *op. cit.*, I, p. 164; and see Stuart to Anson, 17 June 1769 (Staffordshire Record Office, Anson MSS): 'Mrs Montagues room is almost finished.'

44 Stuart to Mrs Montagu, 27 February 1761 (Huntington Library MO 5136).

45 Horace Walpole to William Mason, 14 February 1782 (Walpole, *Correspondence*, ed.W. S. Lewis, XXIX, 1955, p. 184).

46 Blunt, *op. cit.*, II, p. 100.

47 Mrs Montagu to Leonard Smelt, 26 April 1780 (Huntington Library MO 50256).

48   R. and J. Dodsley, *London and its Environs Described*, i, 1761, p. 271. Stuart left intact the Gold Room which had been added at one end of the house by Sir Sampson Gideon's father in the 1750s. This room has been attributed to Isaac Ware on the grounds of its combination of Rococo interior with Palladian exterior, but it now seems that the Rococo plasterwork was added in the early nineteenth century by Lord Saye and Sele.

49   W. Newton, *The Architecture of M. Vitruvius Pollio translated* (ed. J. Newton 1791), Note to Advertisment.

50   The surviving circular pulpit represents the upper stage of a larger construction. Portions of the original rectangular lower storey, ornamented with Coade stone plaques, survive in a store room in the dome of the chapel.

51   Stuart to Bolton, 26 December 1769 (Birmingham City Reference Library, Boulton Papers, S3, no. 274).

52   Stuart to Bolton, Letter Book E, 1771, pp. 161, 211, 212; Letter Book I, 1781, pp. 808, 856, 908 (Birmingham City Reference Library, Boulton Papers); and see R.Rowe, *Adam Silver*, 1965, pl. 47.

53   Stuart to Anson, 4 September 1764 (Staffordshire Record Office, Anson MSS).

54   W. H. St J. Hope, *Windsor Castle*, II, 1913, p. 426.

55   A. P. Oppé, *The Drawings of Paul and Thomas Sandby ... at Windsor Castle*, 1947, pp. 116–17; and S. M. Bond, 'Henry Emlyn of Windsor', *Report of the Society of Friends of St George's Chapel, Windsor*, IV, no. 3, 1962.

56   J. T. Smith, *Nollekens and his Times*, Oxford 1929, p. 27.

57   J. Nichols, *Literary Anecdotes*, IX, p. 146.

58   British Library, Add. MSS 27576, f. 100.

59   *The World* newspaper, 22 February 1788.

60   *Antiquities of Athens*, II, 1787, p. iii.

61   British Library, Add. MSS 27576, f. 9.

List of executed architectural works

WENTWORTH WOODHOUSE, Wentworth, Yorkshire. Interior decoration in the Marble Saloon and elsewhere, e.g. chimney-pieces, from *c.* 1755 for the 2nd Marquess of Rockingham. Today occupied by Sheffield Polytechnic.

HAGLEY HALL, near Stourbridge, West Midlands. Greek Doric temple and four paintings of the Seasons in the drawing room ceiling in 1758–9 for the 1st Lord Lyttelton. Owner: Viscount Cobham. Open to the public: daily from May to September.

SPENCER HOUSE, St James's Place, London. Designed interiors for the 1st Earl Spencer in 1759–65. Now occupied as offices by the Economist Intelligence Unit, and not normally open to the public. Some of Stuart's furniture survives at Althorp, Kenwood, and the Victoria and Albert Museum.

WIMBLEDON HOUSE, Surrey. Interior decoration in *c.* 1758 for the 1st Earl Spencer. Destroyed by fire in 1785.

HOLDERNESSE (later Londonderry) HOUSE, Park Lane, London. Designed interiors and perhaps the house itself in *c.* 1760–5 for the 4th Earl of Holdernesse. Reconstructed by B. D. Wyatt in 1825–8 and demolished in 1964.

GREENWICH HOSPITAL, THE INFIRMARY (now Dreadnought Hospital). 1763–4. A plain building round a courtyard, the western parts damaged by fire in 1811.

LICHFIELD HOUSE, no. 15 St James's Square, London. For Thomas Anson, 1764–6; alterations by S. Wyatt 1791–4. Now occupied as offices by the Clerical, Medical and General Life Assurance Society, and not open to the public.

SHUGBOROUGH, near Stafford, Staffordshire. Stuart's work here for Thomas Anson included alterations to the house, no longer recognisable, and the following buildings in the park: Triumphal Arch, 1764–7; Tower of the Winds, 1764; Greenhouse, 1764, dem. *c.* 1800; Lanthorn of Demosthenes, 1770. He probably also built the Greek Temple and altered the Shepherd's Monument. Owned by the National Trust, administered by Staffordshire County Council, and regularly open to the public.

NUNEHAM PARK, Nuneham Courtenay, Oxfordshire. Designed dining room chimney-piece and drawing room ceiling for the 1st Earl Harcourt in *c.* 1760–4. With the Earl he designed the church, built in the park in 1764. Occupied by Rothmans Ltd. Open to the public.

61

BELVEDERE, near Erith, Kent. House rebuilt for Sir Sampson Gideon *c.* 1775. Dem. 1960.

WIMPOLE HALL, Cambridgeshire. The Prospect House, *c.* 1775. Dem.

MONTAGU (later Portman) HOUSE, Portman Square, London. For Mrs Elizabeth Montagu, *c.* 1775–82. Ballroom executed by Bonomi 1790. Gutted by bombing 1941 and demolished after the war. One of the handsome pairs of gate piers was re-erected at Kenwood, Hampstead, *c.* 1967.

MOUNT STEWART, Co. Down, Ireland. Temple of the Winds, *c.* 1780, for Robert Stewart, 1st Marquis of Londonderry. Owned by the National Trust; regularly open to the public.

GREENWICH HOSPITAL. Chapel rebuilt 1780–8 after fire with assistance of William Newton.

BLITHFIELD HOUSE, Staffordshire. Conservatory for the 1st Lord Bagot built by S. Wyatt from Stuart's designs. Owner: The Lady Bagot.

PARK PLACE, Berkshire. 'Grecian ruins' for General Conway, *c.* 1780. Dem.

Bibliography

PRIMARY SOURCES

J. Stuart, contributions to A. M. Bandini, *De Obelisco Caesaris Augusti*, Rome, 1750.

J. Stuart and N. Revett, *Antiquities of Athens*, 4 vols., 1762–1816 (Stuart contributed the text of the first 2 vols and the notes of the second 2).

There are collections of Stuart's architectural and decorative designs at the Pierpont Morgan Library; the British Museum; the National Maritime Library; and the British Architectural Library, Drawings Collection. This last institution also owns Stuart's topographical drawings in gouache from which the general views in the *Antiquities of Athens* were engraved, as well as his North Italian sketch-book of *c.* 1750 with notes on painting. In the Victoria and Albert Museum (93.D.4) is a book of 100 drawings by John Carter entitled *Drawings made from designs of Flowers & Pateras for Ceilings, Vases, Cornices, Friezes, Architraves, Bases of Columns, Imposts & their Bases, Picture frames, Trophies, Ornaments in Pannells & Parts of different Ceilings. Collected cheifly from Noblemens Houses*, vol. II, 1766. This includes twenty-two interior details of Holdernesse House and two of no. 15 St James's Square.

In the British Museum (Add. MSS 27576) is a memoir of Stuart written by his son James Stuart, RN, in a volume entitled *James Stuart surnamed Athenian*. Further MS material in the British Museum includes *Papers relating to Stuart and Revett's Antiquities of Athens* (Add. MSS 22152) and *Sketches, Plans, etc. illustrative of Stuart and Revett's Antiquities of Athens* (Add. MSS 22153). There are letters by Stuart in the Public Record Office (Add. 65); the Staffordshire County Record Office (Anson MSS D615/P(S)/1/6); the Birmingham City Reference Library (Matthew Boulton papers); Keele University Library; Sheffield Centre Library (Rockingham Papers, R1/70); and the Huntington Library, San Marino (Montagu Collection).

SECONDARY SOURCES

Architectural Publication Society, *Dictionary of Architecture*, VIII, 1887.

Batey, M., 'Nuneham Park, Oxfordshire. The Creation of a Landscape Garden', *Country Life*, 5 September 1968, 540–2.

Blunt, R., ed., *Mrs Montagu, 'Queen of the Blues'*, 2 vols., 1923.

Bolton, A. T., 'James Stuart at Portman House and Spencer House', *Country Life*, 1 May 1915, 6*–11*.

Bolton, A. T., 'Hagley Park', *Country Life*, 16 October 1915, 520–8.

Bolton, A. T., 'Lichfield House, No. 15 St James's Square', *Country Life*, 12 May 1917, 2*–6*.

Caldwell, A., *An Account of the Extraordinary Escape of James Stuart*, 1804 (a broadsheet also printed in *European Magazine*, xlvi, 1804, 369–71).

Chancellor, E. B., *The Private Palaces of London, Past and Present*, 1908.

Clarke, G., 'The Medallions of Concord: an Association between the Society of Arts and Stowe', *Journal of the Royal Society of Arts*, cxxix, no. 5301, August 1981, 611–16.

Colvin, H. M., *A Biographical Dictionary of British Architects 1600–1840*, 1978.

Crook, J. M., *The Greek Revival*, 1972.

Cust, L., and Colvin, S., *History of the Society of Dilettanti*, 1898.

Dictionary of National Biography, lv, 1898.

Fleming, J., *Robert Adam and his Circle in Edinburgh and Rome*, 1962.

'Furniture at Spencer House', *Country Life*, 13 November 1926, 757–9.

Gentleman's Magazine, obituary, 1788, i, 95–6, 216–18.

Goodison, N., 'Mr Stuart's Tripod', *Burlington Magazine*, cxiv, 1972, 695–704.

Goodison, N., *Ormolu: the Work of Matthew Boulton*, 1974.

Halley, J. M. W., 'Lichfield House', *Architectural Review*, May 1910, 273–8.

Hardy, J. and Hayward, H., 'Kedleston Hall, Derbyshire', *Country Life*, 2 February 1978, 262–6.

Harris, E., *The Furniture of Robert Adam*, 1963.

Harris, J., 'Early Neo-Classical Furniture', *Journal of the Furniture History Society*, ii, 1966.

Harris, J., *A Catalogue of British Drawings for Architecture ... in American Collections*, New Jersey, 1971.

Harris, J., 'Newly Acquired Designs by James Stuart in the British Architectural Library, Drawings Collection', *Architectural History*, 22, 1979, 72–7.

Honour, H., 'Adaptations from Athens', *Country Life*, 22 May 1958, 1120–1.

Hussey, C., 'Shugborough, Staffordshire', *Country Life*, 25 Feb., 4–11 March, 15–22 April 1954.

Jourdain, M., 'Furniture, Designed by James Stuart, at Althorp', *Country Life*, 24 August 1935, 204–5.

Kelly, A., *Decorative Wedgwood in Architecture and Furniture*, 1965.

Knight of Glin, *The Temple of the Winds, Mount Stewart*, National Trust guidebook, 1966.

Landy, J., 'Stuart and Revett: Pioneer Archaeologists', *Archaeology*, IX, December 1956, 252–9.

Lawrence [Lewis], L., 'Stuart and Revett: their Literary and Architectural Careers', *Journal of the Warburg Institute*, ii, 1938–9, 128–46.

Lawrence [Lewis], L., 'The Architects of the Chapel at Greenwich Hospital', *Art Bulletin*, xxix, 1947, 260–7.

Lawrence [Lewis], L., 'Greece and Rome at Greenwich', *Architectural Review*, cix, 1951, 17–24.

Bibliography

Lees-Milne, J., 'Shugborough', *Connoisseur*, April–May 1967, 211–15, 4–11.

Memoir of Stuart prefixed to vol. iv of the *Antiquities of Athens*, 1816.

Meteyard, E., *Life of Josiah Wedgwood*, ii, 1866.

Mulvany, J., *Life of James Gandon*, 1846.

Murray, E. Croft, 'A drawing by "Athenian" Stuart for the Painted Room at Spencer House', *British Museum Quarterly*, xxi, 1957, 14–15.

Murray, E. Croft, *Decorative Painting in England 1537–1837*, ii, 1970.

Musgrave, C., *Adam and Hepplewhite and other Neo-Classical Furniture*, 1966.

Nares, G., 'Hagley Hall, Worcestershire', *Country Life*, 19 September 1957, 546–9.

'Nuneham Courtenay Chapel, Oxon.', Supplement to *Architects' Journal*, 18 March and 1 April 1931.

Oswald, A., 'Londonderry House', *Country Life*, 10 July 1937, 38–44.

Papworth, W., 'William Newton and the Chapel of Greenwich Hospital', *RIBA Journal*, xxvii–xxviii, 1891, 417–20.

RIBA Drawings Collection Catalogue, *S*, 1976.

Smith, J. T., *Nollekens and his Times*, 1828.

Spencer, Earl, 'Spencer House', *Country Life*, 6 November 1926, 698–704.

Summerson, J., 'The Society's House: an Architectural Study', *Journal of the Royal Society of Arts*, CII, 1954, 920–33.

Survey of London, xxix–xxx, 1960.

Thornton, P. and Hardy, J., 'The Spencer Furniture at Althorp', *Apollo*, June 1968, 440–51.

Tipping, H. A., 'Wentworth Woodhouse, Yorkshire', *Country Life*, 4 Oct. 1924, 512–19.

Udy, D., 'The Furniture of James Stuart and Robert Adam', *Discovering Antiques*, issue 42, 1971.

Webb, M. I., 'Chimney-pieces by Scheemakers', *Country Life*, 14 March 1957, 491–3.

Wiebenson, D., *Sources of Greek Revival Architecture*, 1969.

Young, A., *A Six Weeks Tour through the Southern Counties of England and Wales*, 2nd. ed., 1769, 354–61.

Index

Adam, James 34
Adam, Robert 31, 32–5, 37, 41, 42, 43, 46, 47, 48, 49, 57; ousts Stuart at Kedleston 33–4; opinion of Stuart 22, 34, 40–1
Althorp, Northamptonshire 35, 36; Stuart furniture at 37, 39–40, *29, 33–8*
Anderson, Diedrich Nicolaus 35
Anson, 1st Lord 20, 25
Anson, Thomas 25–6, 28, 42–3, 55
Antiquities of Athens 15–22, 25, 26, 27, 33, 36, 43, 52, 53, 56, 58, 63, *8, 11–12, 74*
Antiquities of Ionia 54, 56
Athens, Stuart in 18–19; Aqueduct of Hadrian 43, 47; Arch of Hadrian 25, 41, *8*; Erectheion 19, 43, 49, 53, *74*; Monument of Lysicrates 18, 19, 26–7, 33, 34, 39, 44, 53–4, *11–12*, of Thrasyllus 19, 33; Parthenon 15, 19; Propylaea 19; Stoa 19; Temple of Augustus (Gateway of Roman Agora) 19, 29; of Jupiter Olympius 19; on the Ilissus 19, 29; Theseum 23–4; Theatre of Bacchus 19, *5*; Tower of the Winds 18, 19, 26–7, 39, 53
Ayot St Lawrence, Hertfordshire 56–7

Baalbek 18
Babin, J.-P. 15
Bacon, John 53
Bandini, A. M. 14
Belvedere, Kent 46, 47, 48, 51, 60, 62, *64–7*
Benefial, Marco 15
Blenheim, Oxfordshire 23
Blithfield House, Staffordshire 62
Bonomi, Joseph, 29, 49–50, 52, *63*
Borgnis, Pietro Maria 52

Boulton, Matthew 26, 49, 51, 54
Brettingham, Matthew, senior 32–3, 44
Brettingham, Matthew, junior 15, 17, 32–3
Brown, 'Capability' 30
Burke, Edmund 47
Burlington, 3rd Earl of 14, 21

Carrey, Jacques 15
Carter, John 42, 49, *47–50*
'Castor and Pollux', Nollekens' copy of 28
Catton, Charles 53
Chambers, Sir William 21, 57
Chancellor, Edwin Beresford 38
Chandler, Richard 54, 56
Cipriani, Giovanni Battista 49
Clérisseau, Charles-Louis 36
Cobham, 1st Viscount 24, 25
Cockerell, Charles Robert 13
Colbert, Jean-Baptiste 15
Constantinople 19
Conway, General Henry Seymour 30
Curzon, Sir Nathaniel 32–4

Dall, Nicholas Thomas 27
Dance, George, junior 57
Dartmouth, 2nd Earl of 15
Dashwood, Sir Francis 45
Dawkins, James 20
de Bruyn, Theodore 53
de Wailly, Charles 24
Delafosse, Jean-Charles 40
Delos 19
Desgodetz, Antoine 15, 16
Deval, John 53
Dilettanti, Society of 13, 17–18, 20, 25–6, 28, 35, 42, 44–5, 51, 56, 58
Dumont, Gabriel-Pierre-Martin 15

Egremont, 2nd Earl of 15

67

PLATES

1. Self-portrait of Stuart as a youth. He reveals himself as shy and intelligent but scarcely good-looking.

2. Obelisk of Caesar Augustus. Drawn and engraved by Stuart in Rome, 1749, as an early example of etching in the manner of Piranesi.

3. Stables of the Vill Pisani at Stra. From Stuart's Italian sketch-book of 175(

4. Gateway at the Villa Pisani at Stra. From Stuart's Italian sketch-book of 1750.

5. Theatre of Bacchus (or Dionysos), Athens, In this gouache view Stuart shows himself sketching on the right.

6. Doric Temple, Hagley Hall, West Midlands, 1758. The first post-antique use of the Greek Doric order.

7. Triumphal Arch, Shugborough, Staffordshire, 1754–7. Stuart added the elegant urnage and sculpture to the antique original in order to commemorate Admiral and Lady Anson.

9. Tower of the Winds, Shugborough, Staffordshire, 1764. This contains an octagonal coffered dome but the lake which surrounded the building has now disappeared.

8. Arch of Hadrian, from *Antiquities of Athens*, III, 1794. Stuart's view shows how its setting had become as pastoral as that of its imitation at Shugborough.

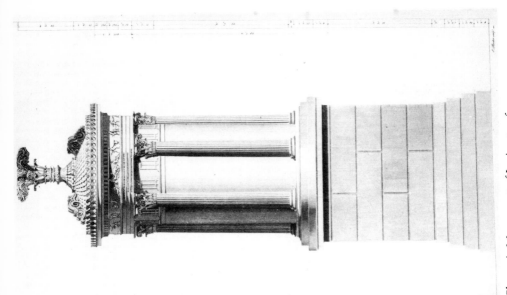

11. Choragic Monument of Lysicrates, from *Antiquities of Athens*, I, 1762. Its succulent

10. Monument of Lysicrates (or Lanthorn of Demosthenes), Shugborough, Staffordshire, 1770. A piquant blend of nature and the antique is provided by the unexpected affinity between the pattern of the

12. Stuart's reconstruction in *Antiquities of Athens*, I, 1762, of the lost tripod from the Choragic Monument of Lysicrates.

13. Shepherd's Monument, Shugborough, Staffordshire, *c*.1758. An eloquent example of the romantic primitivism of the neo-Classical period.

14. A plate from Thomas Wright's *Six Original Designs of Grottos* (1758), which may be related to the design of the Shepherd's Monument at Shugborough.

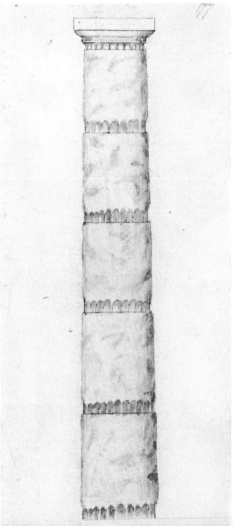

15. Stuart's drawing of an incompletely carved antique column which inspired those of the Shepherd's Monument at Shugborough.

16. Detail of Stuart's chimney-piece at Nuneham Park, Oxfordshire, c.1760. A handsome example of his early and bolder manner.

17. All Saints' church, Nuneham Park, Oxfordshire, designed in 1764 by Stuart and Lord Harcourt. Its austerity of line echoes that of Robert Adam's mausoleum of 1761–4 at Bowood, Wiltshire.

18. Elevational and sectional drawings by Stuart, perhaps an early design for Nuneham church. A Roman Pantheon dome is combined impressively with a Greek Doric order.

19. The Saloon at Wentworth Woodhouse,
South Yorkshire, begun by Flitcroft c.1750, and
adorned by Stuart c.1755 with bas-relief panels
below the gallery.

20–3. Stuart's unexecuted designs for the Great
Saloon at Kedleston, Derbyshire, c.1757.

20. Window wall, with Stuart's characteristic
tripod candelabra and tripod pedestals.

21 Chimney wall The design of the chimney is close to that at Nuneham (pl.16).

22. Sideboard alcove, incorporating a proposed portrait of Sir Nathaniel and Lady Curzon.

23. End wall, with two paintings by Benedetto
Luti flanking a proposed painting inspired by
the frieze on the Choragic Monument of
Lysicrates.

24. Detail from an engraving of *c.*1709 by Chevallier of the gallery at the Louvre of the sculptor Girardon. The imaginary architectural setting is by Oppenord but the objects, including the tripod, are real.

25. Spencer House, London. North and east walls of the Painted Room, 1759. Stuart provided one of the most sumptuous state rooms of eighteenth-century London.

26. Spencer House, London. Screened apse at the south end of the Painted Room, 1759, photographed in 1926 before the dispersal of the contents.

27. Detail from the engraving of the Incantada at Salonica from *Antiquities of Athens*, III, 1794, showing the curved, fluted frieze which Stuart so much admired.

28. Stuart's drawing of 1759 for the north wall of the Painted Room at Spencer House. A rich blend of neo-antique and neo-Renaissance inspiration.

29. Torchère from the Painted Room at Spencer House on its elaborately carved and painted stand.

30. Sofa from the Painted Room at Spencer House. The use of animal parts has a Roman or Hellenistic precedent but Stuart handles them in a somewhat Baroque manner.

31. Spencer House, London. Ballroom, looking north. The room was begun by Vardy in 1756 and decorated in 1764 by Stuart whose high coved ceiling creates the princely air of a Roman *palazzo*.

32. Spencer House, London. North-east corner of the Ballroom. The doorcase, a replica of Stuart's original, dates from a restoration of 1924; note its Incantada frieze.

33. Console table from the Ballroom at Spencer House. Stuart overlays his up-to-date neo-Classical design with neo-Palladian swags.

34. Candle stand from the Painted Room, Spencer House. A striking contrast to the massive quality of the cupboard in pl.35.

35. Night cupboard from Spencer House. An architecturally designed piece demonstrating Stuart's skill and imagination as a furniture designer.

36. Chest from Spencer House. Stuart's perfect statement of the geometrical sobriety of early neo-Classicism.

37 far left. Wardrobe from Spencer House. Stuart's design is here somewhat top-heavy.

38 left. Tripod stand from the Rubens Room, Spencer House. Though comparatively small, this is a commanding object which shows Stuart's early style at its most emphatic.

39. Two designs by Stuart for garlanded pedestals. These show his closeness to contemporary French design.

James Stuart
JH

40 left opposite.
Design by Stuart for
chimney-piece and
overmantel. A
massively
architectural
composition which
adopts the Greek
Doric order in a literal
way which would not
have found favour in
France at this
moment.

41. Design for
decoration of the hall
at Wimbledon House,
c.1758. A bold Doric
scheme and a typical
example of Stuart's
vigorous
impressionistic
drawing technique.

42. Organ case at
Newby Hall, North
Yorkshire. A striking
demonstration of the
close stylistic parallel
between Adam and
Stuart in the 1760s.

43. Design for a chimney-piece by Stuart. Its elegant attenuation is reminiscent of the organ case at Newby Hall.

44. Holdernesse House, London. North drawing room. Stuart's ceiling of c.1760–5 seems to be inspired by Adam.

45. Holdernesse House, London. Centre drawing room, c.1760–5. Stuart's ceiling is inspired by the florid marble ceiling in the southern shrine of the Temple of the Sun (or Bel) at Palmyra as illustrated in Robert Wood's *The Ruins of Palmyra, otherwise Tedmor, in the Desert*, 1753, pl.XIX.

46. Holdernesse House, London. Boudoir, c.1760–5. The massive coffered cove recurred in Stuart's Montagu House and Belvedere.

Ornament, in a Ceiling at Lord Holdernesses.

Stuart dir.

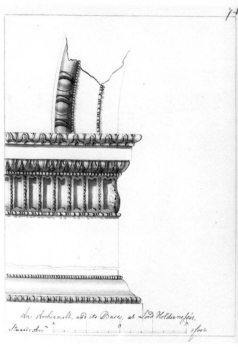

An Archivault, and its Bases, at Lord Holdernesses.

Stuart dir.

47. Coffering with enriched guilloche borders in the Boudoir.

48. Detail of the springing of an arch similar to that at Montagu House (pl.61).

A Flower, in a Ceiling at Lord Holdernesses' Park lane.

Stuart dir.

Entablature at Lord Holdernesses.

Stuart dir.

49. Ornamental patera from a plaster ceiling.

50. Anthemion frieze inspired by the Erectheion in Athens.

47–50. Holdernesse House, London. 4 drawings by John Carter, 1766, of decorative details.

51. 15 St James's Square, London, 1764–6. Stuart's crisp Palladian entrance front is enlivened with Grecian detail. S. Wyatt lengthened the first-floor windows and added the iron balcony in the 1790's.

52. 15 St James's Square, London, 1764–6. First-floor front drawing room. Stuart's ceiling is inspired by the heavy proto-Baroque ceiling in the Temple of the Sun at Palmyra of the first century AD (cf.pl.45).

53. 15 St James's Square, London, 1764–6. Chimney-piece in the first-floor front drawing room. With its Lysicrates frieze this is similar to Stuart's chimney-piece from the Ballroom at Spencer House now in the Picture Gallery at Althorp, Northamptonshire.

54. Montagu House, London, c.1775–82. The arch of the Venetian window descends through the frieze as at the Aqueduct of Hadrian in Athens. The porte-cochère is a Victorian addition.

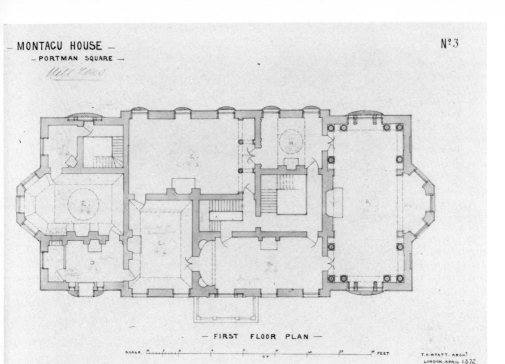

MONTAGU HOUSE
PORTMAN SQUARE

— FIRST FLOOR PLAN —

55. Montagu House, London, c.1775–82. First-floor plan. The circuit of five intercommunicating reception rooms for Mrs Montagu's celebrated parties or salons opens off the main staircase. Her private rooms are on the left at the south-west end of the house.

56. Montague House, London, c. 1775–82. Cross-sections drawn, like the plan, by T.H.Wyatt in 1872 as part of a survey made shortly before the property reverted to the Portman family.

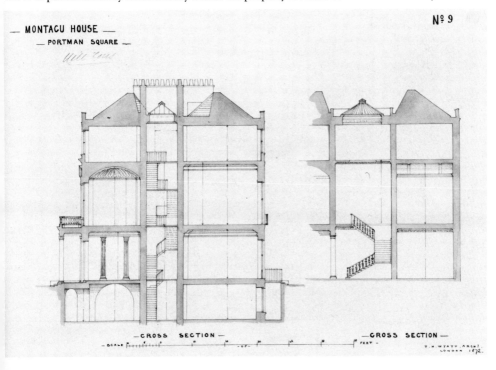

MONTAGU HOUSE
PORTMAN SQUARE

— CROSS SECTION —   — CROSS SECTION —

58. Montagu House, London, c.1775–82. The Ionic hall of what Walpole described as 'a noble simple edifice'.

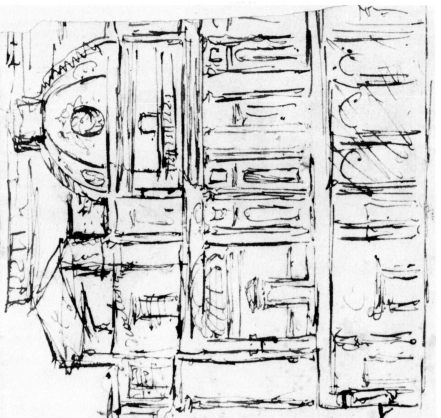

57. Part-section of a rotunda-type house. This suggests that Stuart could design a more imaginative house on paper than in reality.

59. Montagu House, London, c.1775–82. Morning room. The elaborate ceiling combined some of the favourite motifs of Stuart and Adam.

60. Montagu House, London, *c*.1775–82. Reception room (marked 'B' on the plan in pl.55). A brilliant essay in the Adam style.

61. Montagu House, London, c.1775–82. Drawing room (marked 'G' on the plan in pl.55). The grace of Stuart's ornament is obscured by the Late Victorian furnishings.

62. Montagu House, London, *c*.1775–90. Ballroom (marked 'A' on the plan in pl.55). This splendid interior has a Roman *gravitas* unlike the work of Adam.

63. Montagu House, London. Bonomi's drawing for the completion of the Ballroom, 1790.

64. Belvedere, Kent, *c.*1775. A plain façade like that of Montagu House. The original entrance front of the Georgian house which Stuart remodelled and extended occupied the site of the left-hand façade in this view.

65. Belvedere, Kent, *c.*1775. Detail of the Venetian window and lunette on the rear façade. Once again Stuart's arch springs from the frieze not from the crowning cornice of the whole entablature as had been the case in the Venetian windows designed by Lord Burlington and his followers.

66. Chimney-piece of the late 1780s formerly at Belvedere, Kent. The animated naturalism of Stuart's neo-antique plant ornament is offset by Wedgwood's gem-like jasper plaques.

67. Detail of the chimney-piece shown in pl.66.

68. Greenwich Hospital Chapel, rebuilt by Stuart and Newton, 1779–90. North side looking East. This shows the parts which, according to Newton, were designed by Stuart: ceiling, gallery balusters and altar-piece frame.

69. Greenwich Hospital Chapel, rebuilt by Stuart and Newton, 1779–90. Detail of the gallery with anthemion frieze and sumptuous brackets.

70. Greenwich Hospital Chapel, rebuilt by Stuart and Newton, 1779–90. Contract drawing of 1782, probably by Newton, for t decoration of the west end.

72. Ionic capital from the Erectheion as depicted in *Antiquities of Athens*, II, 1789.

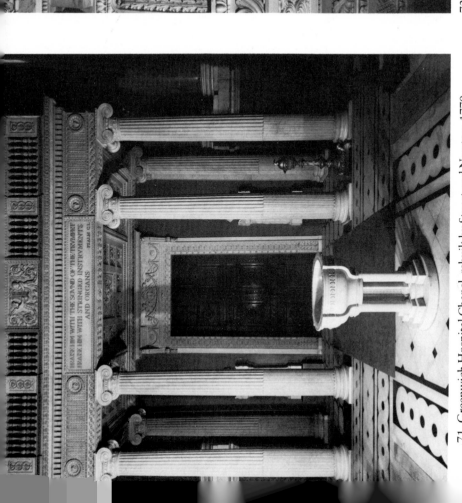

71. Greenwich Hospital Chapel, rebuilt by Stuart and Newton, 1779–90. Organ screen at the west end, showing the substitution of Stuart's favourite Erectheion Ionic order in place of the lotus capitals shown in the contract drawings (pl.70).

73. Greenwich
Hospital Chapel,
rebuilt by Stuart and
Newton, 1779–90.
Working drawing,
made in Stuart's
office, for the capitals
on the organ screen.
The bead and reel
moulding at the base
was omitted in
execution.

74. Greenwich
Hospital Chapel,
rebuilt by Stuart and
Newton, 1779–90.
Detail of a capital and
its entablature on the
organ screen: the final
stage in the
translation into
marble of the
engraving in the
Antiquities of Athens.

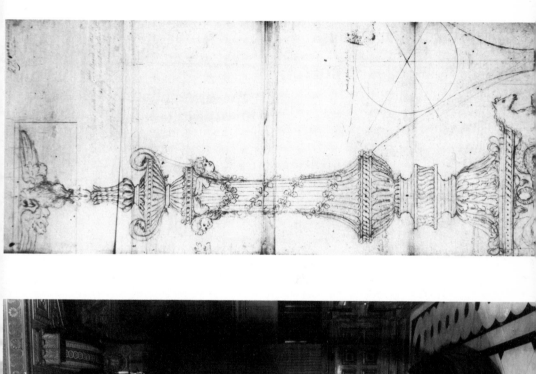

75. Pulpit from
Greenwich Hospital
Chapel, 1788. An
exceptionally
imaginative use of a
Hellenistic source.

76. Drawing by
Newton for the
wooden lectern at
Greenwich Hospital
Chapel. This fanciful
object is a pair to the
font shown in pl.77.

77. Font at Greenwich Hospital Chapel. We know from his working drawings that Newton submitted his design for the candelabra to Stuart for his comments; he presumably did the same with his designs for the lectern and font.

78. Drawing by Stuart for an ornamental composition perhaps related to a design for a medal. Stuart's exuberant style influenced designs by Newton such as those for the lectern and font at Greenwich Hospital Chapel.

A Design for
The east end of S! George Chapel.

80. Design for east end of St George's Chapel, Windsor, 1771. Stuart's monstrous essay in Georgian Gothick was not executed.

79. Monument to the 1st Earl of Hardwicke and his wife, Wimpole church, Cambridgeshire. Designed by Stuart, 1764, and executed by P. Scheemakers, 1766. The noble figure of Minerva (or Athene) on the right is a fine example of Stuart's Augustan adaptation of